❧ Beadwork Inspired by Art ❧

ART NOUVEAU

Creative Publishing international

First published in the United States of America by

Creative Publishing international, Inc., a member of
Quayside Publishing Group
400 First Avenue North
Suite 300
Minneapolis, MN 55401
1-800-328-3895
www.creativepub.com

ISBN-13: 978-1-58923-388-1
ISBN-10: 1-58923-388-3

10 9 8 7 6 5 4 3 2 1

Library of Congress Cataloging-in-Publication Data

Durant, Judith, 1955-
  Beadwork inspired by art : Art Nouveau jewelry and
accessories / by Judith Durant and Jean Campbell.
     p. cm.
  ISBN 978-1-58923-388-1
  1. Beadwork. 2. Art nouveau. 3. Jewelry making.
  I. Campbell, Jean, 1964- II. Title.
  TT860.D867 2008
  745.58'2--dc22

                          2008018060

Cover and Book Design: Everlution Design
Page Layout: Everlution Design
Illustrations: Julia S. Pretl
Photographs: Glenn Scott Photography
Copy Editor: Amy Fletcher
Proofreader: Karen Ruth
Cover photo: Galeries Lafayette Dome (Archive Timothy McCarthy / Art Resource, NY)

Printed in Singapore

Beadwork Inspired by Art

ART NOUVEAU

JEWELRY AND ACCESSORIES

JUDITH DURANT ✿ JEAN CAMPBELL

Creative Publishing
international

contents

introduction

INSPIRED BY THE GREAT MASTERPIECES of fine artists—and working with a vast array of beads and numerous techniques from stringing to weaving—beadworkers can produce their own works of art. A fine artist might work with paint and canvas while a beadworker "paints" with beads and thread, but both use color, texture, and design to create unique works of art.

As beadworkers ourselves, we're both always hungry to learn more ways to work with color and texture. So we decided to look to the masters for inspiration. In *Beadwork Inspired by Art: Art Nouveau Jewelry and Accessories*, we explore the decorative art style that exploded onto the scene of every-day life at the turn of the twentieth century. This period is particularly appealing to us because, like us, Art Nouveau artists were decorating everything in sight—whether it needed it or not! We picked some of our favorite works from this period, spent time with them at home and at the bead store, and let them be our muses as we designed the twelve projects you'll find in this book.

We discovered that just as there are many ways to interpret a sunset, a still life, or a flight of imagination into a work of art, so there are also many ways to interpret a work of art into bead-work. We took a somewhat literal approach to recreating part of an artwork for *Libussa Bracelet* on page 14, *Métro Station Earrings* on page 22, and *The Embrace Vase* on page 26. We focused on color and texture for *Casa Milà Necklace* on page 18 and *Nouveau Tilework Necklace* on page 62. The interpretation of mood and color also led us to create *Scheherazade Necklace* on page 56 and *Villa Igiea Palermo Necklace* on page 68.

As you flip through the book you'll find clear step-by-step instructions to make each design. The detailed illustrations will help you get the job done, too. If you're new to a technique or maybe a little rusty, check pages 84–92 for all the background information you'll need to know.

We hope that by creating these projects, you'll learn a little more about how to work with color and texture in your own designs. And wearing beadwork inspired by a work of art is a conversa-tion just waiting to happen! Who knows? You may soon be paging through art books yourself and finding inspiration for your own beaded masterpieces.

about art nouveau

Art Nouveau, which means "new art" in French, is a style of art, design, and architecture that developed across Western Europe and North America in the late nineteenth century and ended at the onset of World War I in 1914. First seen in London as early as 1880, the style took its name from a shop in Paris called Maison de l'Art Nouveau, which opened in 1896 to exhibit works in this new style. Characterized during its early phase by flowing lines and curves—often in the form of flowers, vines, and leaves, and later in more geometric, rectilinear, and cubic forms—the style was used in architecture, interior design, jewelry, sculpture, and glassworks in addition to paintings, illustrations, and posters. Artists applied the style to everything from buildings and furniture to textiles and clothes.

The Art Nouveau style may have grown in part as a response to the Industrial Revolution, with artists responding to the low standards of mass production by applying their design skills and artisanship to articles of everyday life. Entryways to the Paris Métro became works of art at the hands of French artist and architect Hector Guimard. Lamps, vases, wine goblets, and all manner of stained glass were sensuously shaped and colored by the world-renowned American artist and designer Louis Comfort Tiffany. Posters created by Henri de Toulouse-Lautrec, advertising the Moulin Rouge in the Montmartre neighborhood of Paris, beckoned passersby to come to the cabaret.

Artists working during this period sought to create a new art form that elevated all craftsmanship to the level of "art" and eschewed the classical and traditional art that was prevalent through the mid-nineteenth century.

They turned to nature for inspiration, but rather than strive for realistic interpretations, artists stressed the linear and abstract qualities of vegetation.

At the same time, the goal of Art Nouveau was to create art that centered on people and their lives. Although they believed that furniture should be made for practical use, artists of the Art Nouveau period also believed it should be decorated for pleasure, with the decoration derived from nature. The water lily was transformed into a side table by Émile Gallé. A cabinet by Louis Majorelle has a tree "growing" right up its front. Alphonse Mucha featured poppies in a wallpaper design. Blossoms and plants made with pearls and semiprecious stones found their way into the fine jewelry of René Lalique. Although a specific form of flora may not be discernable in all of Antoni Gaudí's architecture, writhing plant forms are abundant on his balconies and facades, and there is no mistaking the influence of plant life on the swirling glasswork of Tiffany.

Construction of the signature undulating and whiplash curves of the Art Nouveau style was made possible in part by the new technology and materials of the very movement that Art Nouveau artists were reacting to: the Industrial Revolution. Cast iron, for example, which was produced in a blast furnace and used for columns in the building industry, was manipulated into elaborate shapes by Hector Guimard and others. Possibly in reaction to the development of the glass-pressing machine in 1827, which allowed mass production of cheap glass products, Tiffany and others crafted one-of-a-kind handcrafted masterpieces in glass.

Métro Station Entrance

The entrance to the Porte Dauphine
Paris Métro station is one of the
last existing examples of the Art
Nouveau stations designed
by Hector Guimard.
(ERICH LESSING / ART RESOURCE, NY)

In Europe, Brussels was a hub for
the new art in the 1880s and 1890s,
where the art review *L'Art Moderne*
was founded in 1881. The publication
was important for the exchange of
ideas between artists from different
countries. Significant Art Nouveau
artists from Belgium include architect,
interior designer, and furniture designer Victor Horta, who made a cast-iron
door handle for the Solvay residence in
Brussels come alive with camber; and
Henry van de Velde, architect, interior
decorator, furniture designer, graphic
artist, and writer, who added sumptuous curves to everything from buildings to women's dresses.

In France, a new architecture flaunted the Art Nouveau
style through the designs of Guimard. True to the goal
of incorporating art into everyday life, his elaborate
entryways and pavilions for the Métro are more about
art than the fact that they lead to public transportation.
Émile Gallé applied skills gleaned from his father's glass
and pottery workshop to produce unique Art Nouveau
glassware that combined subtle coloring techniques and
delicate botanical forms.

Toulouse-Lautrec produced some of the most widely rec-
ognizable examples of paintings and posters true to the
style, including the billowing cancan dancers he created
to advertise France's dance troupes.

The German term for Art Nouveau is *Jugendstil*. In
Austria, it is known as *Sezessionsstil*, and the word
Modernisme describes the style in Spain. The Jugendstil
movement began in Germany with an exhibition of

Poster for the Moulin Rouge
Henri de Toulouse-Lautrec's 1893 poster advertisement for the Moulin Rouge cabaret in the Montmarte section of Paris, France. (GIRAUDON / ART RESOURCE, NY)

embroideries by Hermann Obrist. His tapestry of stylized cyclamen epitomizes the use of exaggerated curves, which is reflected in the title of the work, *Whiplash*. The borders and frames of German artist Max Klinger are representative of the Jugendstil style with its use of stylized peonies, doves, and vines, which were used to decorate book pages. Sezessionsstil art in Vienna is best known through the works of Gustav Klimt. Working with the female body as his primary subject,

Klimt produced paintings and murals that, rather than using plant life as the basic form, used instead all manner of geometrics—such as squares, circles, and spirals, perhaps initiating the geometric period of Art Nouveau. Paint thick with gold and silver added relief to his canvases, and his paintings are a confluence of ancient Egyptian symbolism and the most modern techniques.

Some people say that the outstanding genius of the entire international Art Nouveau movement was Spain's Modernisme architect Antoni Gaudí. He developed a highly original style, one that has been described as the integration of nature's organic shapes and the fluidity of water. The culmination of his life's work was the church La Sagrada Família in Barcelona, in which he elaborately decorated every nave, nook, and crypt. Gaudí dedicated most of his working life to this endeavor, but he was unfortunately killed in an accident before its completion.

London is said to be the birthplace of Art Nouveau, and it was home to Aubrey Vincent Beardsley, a musician, draftsman, and writer who made a significant mark on the Art Nouveau world in his short, twenty-six-year-long life. His drawing talents were in demand in the world of publishing, where he produced posters, illustrations, and even a binding for Oscar Wilde's famous play *Salome*. Also active on the London Art Nouveau scene was Charles Ricketts, whose illustrations were published in many books. Elsewhere in Great Britain, the heart of Art Nouveau lay mainly in the hands of Scottish architect, designer, and artist Charles Rennie Mackintosh. He applied the Art Nouveau style to buildings, most notably the Glasgow School of Art, which exhibits sublime harmony between the straight lines of stone building construction and the curvaceous lines of cast-iron decoration.

In the United States, the movement was represented mainly in the works of architect Louis Sullivan and glassware designer Louis Comfort Tiffany. Although Sullivan's buildings are not designed in the Art Nouveau style, the stone and metal surfaces employ both the organic lines of the early style and the exaggerated geometric signatures of the later style. Tiffany's goblets and lamps exhibited all of the requisite curves of the period, and the lamps are imitated and produced in great quantity to this day.

Another significant artist working in the Art Nouveau style was Alphonse Mucha from Moravia, which is now part of the modern Czech Republic. In Mucha's works, such as *The Seasons*, the female forms are as sinuous, soft, and flowing as the seasonal foliage that surrounds them.

Many other artists' contributions helped define Art Nouveau, a movement still visible in everyday life. The next time you're in Paris, go to Galeries Lafayette and look up at the glass dome designed by Ferdinand Chanut and Georges Chedanne. In Buffalo, New York, you can marvel at Louis Sullivan's main entrance of the Guaranty Building. Walk through Henry van de Velde's entrance to the Werkbund Theatre in Cologne, Germany, and you'll be transported back in time. Although they produced their work over a relatively short period of time, Art Nouveau artists were prolific, and they left their mark in many surprising places.

INSPIRING ARTISTS *of the* ART NOUVEAU PERIOD

LEON BAKST *(1866–1924)*

ERNESTO BASILE *(1857–1932)*

AUBREY VINCENT BEARDSLEY *(1872–1898)*

FERDINAND CHANUT *(1872–1961)*

GEORGES CHEDANNE *(1861–1940)*

ÉMILE GALLÉ *(1846–1904)*

ANTONI GAUDÍ *(1852–1926)*

HECTOR GUIMARD *(1867–1942)*

JOSEF HOFFMANN *(1870–1956)*

VICTOR HORTA *(1861–1947)*

GUSTAV KLIMT *(1862–1918)*

RENÉ LALIQUE *(1860–1945)*

CHARLES RENNIE MACKINTOSH *(1868–1928)*

VITEZLAV KAREL MASEK *(1865–1927)*

ALPHONSE MUCHA *(1860–1939)*

HERMANN OBRIST *(1863–1927)*

CHARLES RICKETTS *(1866–1933)*

THÉOPHILE ALEXANDRE STEINLEN *(1859–1923)*

FRANZ VON STUCK *(1863–1928)*

LOUIS SULLIVAN *(1856–1924)*

LOUIS COMFORT TIFFANY *(1848–1933)*

HENRI DE TOULOUSE-LAUTREC *(1864–1901)*

HENRY VAN DE VELDE *(1863–1957)*

projects

Libussa Bracelet

Libussa

Vitezlav Karel Masek was painting in Czechoslovakia during the height of the Art Nouveau movement. This painting, entitled *Libussa*, is of the legendary Bohemian princess more commonly known as Libuse, who is said to have founded the city of Prague. Painted in 1893, the oil on canvas work now resides in the Musée d'Orsay in Paris, France.

THIS MOODY, SOMEWHAT SURREAL painting by Vitezlav Karel Masek has many elements typical of the Art Nouveau style: elaborate decorative elements in gold, a bouquet of leaves, beautiful curving lines, and plenty of mystery. The center strip of the princess Libussa's gown was easily translated into a bracelet of colorful glass beads enveloped in gold, then surrounded by ivory.

FINISHED LENGTH:

7¼" (18.5 cm) including clasp

TECHNIQUES:

square stitch

MATERIALS AND TOOLS

· size 11° seed beads: 3 g ivory,
  1 g metallic gold

· 6mm round glass beads: 4 each
  red, ivory, topaz, blue

· 5mm thin gold daisy spacers (32)

· 10mm two-hole gold box clasp (1)

· 6-lb. test braided beading thread

· scissors

· size 12 beading needle

1 Thread a needle with approximately 3' (1 m) of thread and wax well. Pick up eleven 11° ivory seed beads. Continuing with ivory seed beads, work three rows of square stitch eleven beads wide—you will have four rows total.

2 Working one side of the bracelet only, work sixty-five rows of square stitch three beads wide (**figure 1**).

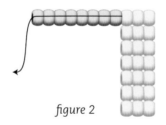

figure 1

3 Exiting from the outside bead in the last row, work three more beads in square stitch, then string eight seed beads (**figure 2**).

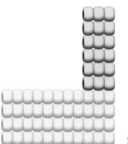

figure 2

4 Keeping the tension tight, work square stitch back across the eleven seed beads. Continuing with ivory seed beads, work two more rows of square stitch. This is one end of the bracelet.

Note: In order for the picot edging to come out even, you need an even number of rows down the length of the bracelet, so this end has one fewer row than the opposite end.

5 Weave back down through the work so the thread exits from the last bead in the first eleven-bead row at this first end of the bracelet. Work sixty-five rows of square stitch three beads wide (**figure 3**).

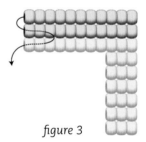

figure 3

6 Join the last row to the outside three beads of the next eleven-bead row (**figure 4**).

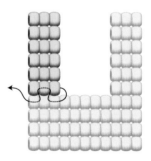

figure 4

7 Weave through the work to the first eleven-bead row. Work two rows of square stitch, decreasing one stitch at the beginning and end of each row. The last row is seven beads wide.

8 To attach the first half of the clasp, exit the inside of an end bead. Pass the needle several times around the thread between this end bead and the one next to it. Pick up two metallic seed beads, pass through one hole in the clasp, pick up two metallic seed beads. *Pass the needle around the thread between the two end beads and through the two metallic seed beads, the clasp, and the two metallic seed beads just strung. Repeat from * several times **(figure 5)**.

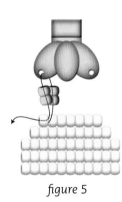

figure 5

Exiting between the last two beads at the other side, attach the other end of this half of the clasp.

9 Exiting from the inside of the first three-bead row on one side, pick up five metallic seed beads and pass through two beads of the opposite three-bead row. Weave through the beadwork and exit from the third inside bead on this side **(figure 6)**.

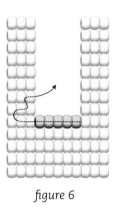

figure 6

10 Pick up one spacer, one 6mm bead, and one spacer. Pass through one or more beads of the opposite three-bead row.

Continue in this manner, alternating five gold seed beads and spacer/6mm/spacer between every third row. When you reach the other end of the bracelet, weave through to the last eleven-bead row and repeat steps 7 and 8, attaching the other half of the clasp to this end of the bracelet **(figure 7)**.

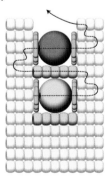

figure 7

11 To add the picot edge, exit from the last bead of an end row. *Pick up one metallic seed bead and pass through the last bead of the next row. Repeat from * one more time **(figure 8)**.

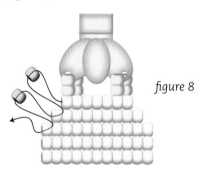

figure 8

Exiting from the end bead of an eleven-bead row, pick up one metallic, one ivory, and one metallic seed bead. Pass down through two beads in the next row. Repeat from ** to the last eleven-bead row, then add one metallic seed bead at the end of the last two rows as before **(figure 9).

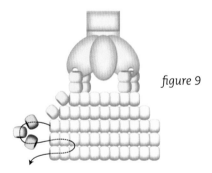

figure 9

12 Repeat step 11 to embellish the other side of the bracelet. Weave in all ends and trim threads close to the beadwork.

Casa Milà Necklace

Casa Milà

Antoni Plàcid Guillem Gaudí Cornet was born in Reus (Catalonia), Spain, in 1852. A sick child who couldn't regularly attend school, he spent much of his childhood convalescing in the country. This early, intimate exposure to nature was a catalyst for his fascination with organic forms, about which he said, "Everything comes from the great book of nature." Sometimes called a Gothic Surrealist, Gaudí was considered the chief architect of the Spanish Art Nouveau movement. Casa Milà, also known as La Pedrera, was constructed between 1906 and 1910.

(Vanni / Art Resource, NY)

THE LINKED BEADED BEADS IN THIS simple necklace echo the undulating forms of Antoni Gaudí's Casa Milà, an apartment building he designed in Barcelona, Spain. The necklace's muted colors imitate the chipped-stone exterior of the building, and the focal pendant lends an organic element. All combine to evoke the fanciful feel of the architect's work.

FINISHED LENGTH:

18 ½" (47 cm)

TECHNIQUES:

ladder stitch, tubular herringbone stitch, stringing, crimping

MATERIALS AND TOOLS

- size 11° true-cut seed beads, 10 g metallic silver

- size 11° cylinder beads, 10 g gunmetal

- size 10° hex-cut seed beads, 10 g taupe

- size 8° seed beads, 10 g silver

- 6mm crystal bicones (24), smoke

- 3.5mm Thai silver faceted cubes (12)

- 5 x 7mm Thai silver wide-holed rondelles with design (2)

- 4 x 9mm Thai silver triangular tubes with design (4)

- 17 x 26mm fine silver pendant with horizontal hole (1)

- 2 x 2mm sterling silver crimp tubes (2)

- Thai silver S clasp with rings (1)

- 6-lb. test braided beading thread

- flexible beading wire (22" [56 cm])

- size 12 beading needle

- scissors

- crimping pliers

- wire cutters

1 Thread the needle with approximately 3' (1 m) of thread. Leaving a 4" (10 cm) tail, use cylinder beads to make a strip of ladder stitch eight beads long. Work a final ladder stitch to connect the first and last beads added to make a ring. This is round 1 **(figure 1)**.

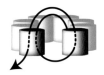

figure 1

2 Work tubular herringbone stitch off the ladder-stiched base **(figure 2)**. For round 2 use cylinder beads; rounds 3 and 4, true-cuts; round 5, hex-cuts; round 6, 6° seed beads; round 7, hex-cuts; rounds 8 and 9, true-cuts; rounds 10 and 11, cylinder beads.

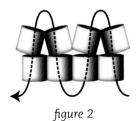

figure 2

3 Weave through the beads added in round 11 in a ladder-stitched thread path to tighten the beaded bead and mimic round 1 (Figure 3). Weave through all the beads several times to reinforce. Secure the thread and trim **(figure 3)**. Set aside.

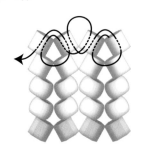

figure 3

4 Repeat steps 1 to 3 seven more times to make a total of eight beaded beads.

5 Use one crimp tube to connect the beading wire to one-half of the clasp. String on one silver rondelle and slide it over the crimp tube.

6 String on a sequence of one crystal, one hex-cut, one cube, one hex-cut, one crystal, one hex-cut, one triangular tube, and one hex-cut twice. String on a sequence of one crystal, one hex-cut, one cube, one hex-cut, one crystal, and one beaded bead three times. String on one crystal, one hex-cut, one cube, one hex-cut, one crystal, one beaded bead, one crystal, one hex-cut, and two true-cuts. String on the pendant and repeat the step in reverse.

7 String on one rondelle, one crimp tube, and the other half of the clasp. Pass back through the crimp tube and rondelle. Let the strand hang vertically and pull the wire tight to snug all the beads. The crimp tube should sit right at the edge of the rondelle without sliding into it. Crimp the tube. When the necklace is worn, the rondelle should cover the crimp tube just added. Trim any excess wire.

BEADED BEAD VARIATIONS

The beaded beads featured in *Casa Milà Necklace* are shaped not by fancy stitching, but by simply increasing and decreasing bead sizes in each round. Using the same basic herringbone-stitched pattern and the exact same beads, you can make your own shapes by varying the rounds in which you use different bead sizes. Try these examples to start and then branch out to experiment on your own.

Two rounds with 8° beads, one with hex beads, two with 11° beads, one with cylinder beads, two with 11° beads, one with hex beads, and two with 8° beads makes an *hourglass* shape.

One round with hex beads, two with 11° beads, five with cylinder beads, two with 11° beads, and one with hex beads makes a *patterned tube*.

Two rounds with 8° beads, nine with alternating 8° beads and cylinder beads, and one with 8° beads makes a *cone*.

One round with all cylinder beads makes a *tight tube*.

hourglass   *patterned tube*   *cone*   *tight tube*

Métro Station Earrings

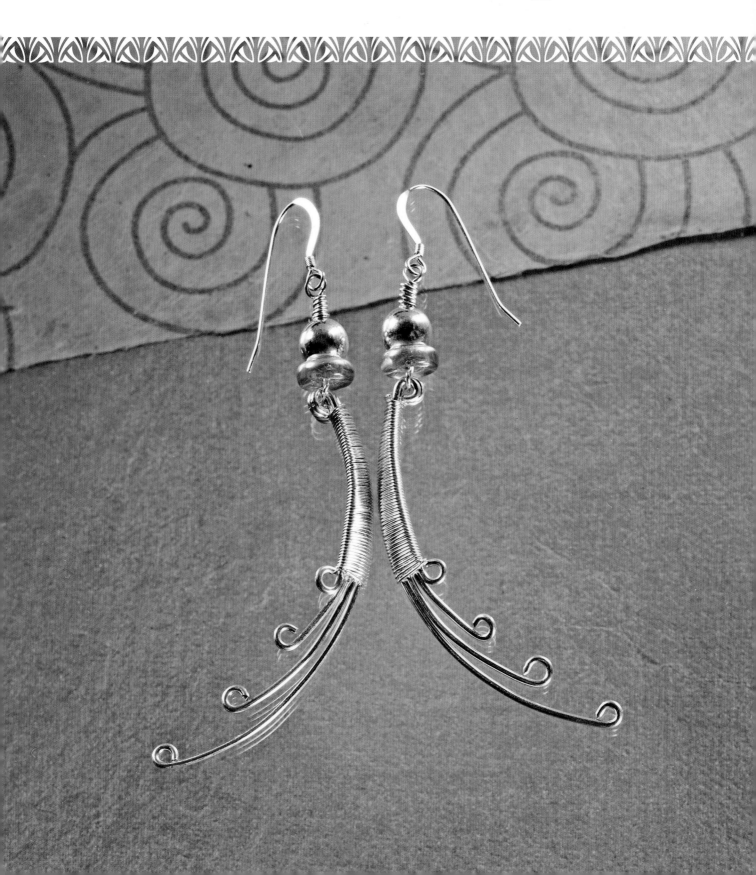

THE DISTINCTIVE METAL CURVES in this detail from a Guimard métro station in Paris are reflected in these wireworked earrings. A fashionable Parisienne of the day would find these earrings irresistible, as they would nicely complement a long slinky dress, tiara, and voluminous, colorful wrap.

FINISHED LENGTH:

2 ¾" (7 cm)

TECHNIQUES:

wrapped loop, wire wrapping

MATERIALS AND TOOLS

- 7mm sterling silver seamless rounds (2)

- 3 x 8mm silver glass wide-holed spacers (2)

- sterling silver ear wires (2)

- 24-gauge sterling silver wire (50" [1.5 m])

- 20-gauge sterling silver wire (25" [63.5 cm])

- wire cutters

- round-nose pliers

- chain-nose pliers

1 Cut one 3 ½" (9 cm), one 2 ¾" (7 cm), one 2 ¼" (5.7 cm), and one 1 ¾" (4.5 cm) piece of 20-gauge wire, keeping the natural curve intact.

2 Use chain-nose pliers to grasp the tip of one of the wires. Roll your wrist toward the inside of the wire's curve until the wire touches itself, forming a P shape. Repeat to form loops at each end of each wire. Set aside.

3 Cut a 25" (63.5 cm) length of 24-gauge wire and set aside.

4 Gather the 20-gauge looped wires together. Slide the wires so the loops at the base end are even and in descending-length order. Let the loops at the other end fan out (**figure 1**).

5 Wrap the end of the 24-gauge wire around the base end loops. Continue to grasp the 20-gauge wires firmly in one hand, maintaining the fan at one end, as you use the other hand to tightly and evenly wrap the 24-gauge wire down to meet the simple loop of the shortest piece of 20-gauge wire. Trim any excess wire close to the wraps. Set the fan aside (**figure 2**).

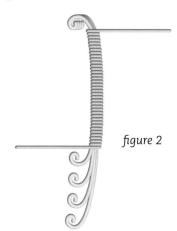

figure 2

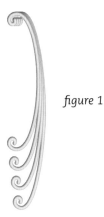

figure 1

6 Cut a 2" (5 cm) length of 20-gauge wire. Pass one end through the loops at the base end of the fan so the wire end sticks out ½" (1.5 cm). Cross the wire ends across the top of the loops, then bend them straight up **(figure 3)**.

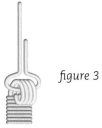

figure 3

7 String one spacer and one round onto the paired wires.

8 Use the long wire end to form a wrapped loop that incorporates the short wire end **(figure 4)**.

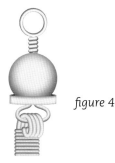

figure 4

9 Attach an ear wire to the wrapped loop.

10 Repeat all steps to make a second earring.

CLEAN WIREWORK

Making clean wire loops and coils is a key component to giving *Métro Station Earrings* a professional look. Here are four tips to put you on your way.

1. Use flush cutters to trim the wire ends so they are perfectly flat. This way, when making simple loops, you can make the wire end sit flat against itself, making a clean, visually even line.

2. Take your time while you wrap. If you work slowly, you can ensure that the wraps touch sides, making a perfect coil. If the wraps are even a little bit off, immediately make an adjustment, as a small mistake at the beginning ends up throwing off the whole coil.

3. Use not only your pliers, but your fingers to straighten, shape, and manipulate the wire.

4. Use chain-nose pliers to gently squeeze the cut end of the wire against the coil, tucking it out of the way. Use a metal file to remove any sharp edges.

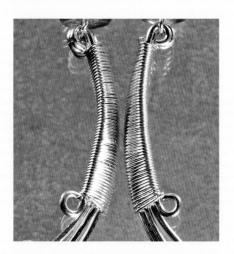

The Embrace Vase

The Embrace

Gustav Klimt was born in Baumgarten, Austria, in 1862, and became one of the most prominent artists in the Vienna Art Nouveau movement. His father was a gold engraver, which may have influenced the frequent use of gold and silver in his paintings. *The Embrace* is a sketch for the frieze at the Palais Stoclet in Brussels. Painted from 1905 to 1909, the sketch is made with watercolor and pencil and measures 77" x 47" (194.6 x 120.3 cm). It is currently housed at the Museum für Angewandte Kunst in Vienna, Austria.

(Scala / Art Resource, NY)

THE GOLD AND SILVER geometric forms of Gustav Klimt are compelling. Although they are very orderly, they appear spontaneous, rendering the painting both formal and casual in form at the same time. This dual effect is the intention of the beaded vase—although it presents crisp lines and a symmetrical shape, the beadwork is malleable and the form can be tweaked. This vase was woven on a loom, but it could also be woven with square stitch.

FINISHED SIZE:

6" (15 cm) tall and 4.5" (11.5 cm) wide at base

TECHNIQUES:

loomwork, loomwork decreases and increases

MATERIALS AND TOOLS

- size 11° cylinder beads: approximately 41 g nickel plated, 33 g black, 17 g metallic gunmetal, 10 g light bronze

- bead loom

- size D nylon thread, black

- size 12 beading needle

- beeswax or thread conditioner

- scissors

1 Prepare the loom with eighty warp threads. Thread a needle with 3' (1 m) of thread, wax well, and tie the end to the leftmost warp thread near the bottom of the loom. Beginning with the bottom row of chart 1 on page 30, pick up seventy-nine beads, following the pattern from left to right. Complete this row, then work rows 2 and 3 in the same manner, each with seventy-nine beads.

2 To begin row 4, weave through the work to put your thread in position to decrease one bead (page 88), string seventy-seven beads following the pattern from left to right, and bring the needle up between the last two warp threads. Complete the row and work row 5 evenly with seventy-seven beads.

3 Continue following chart 1 for bead sequence and shaping, both increasing and decreasing accordingly. Cut the piece from the loom, leaving threads long enough to weave back into the work. Re-warp the loom and make a second piece following chart 1 again.

4 Work steps 1 through 3 again, this time following chart 2 on page 31.

5 Prepare the loom with sixty-five warp threads. Beginning with the bottom row of chart 3 below, string sixty-four beads, following the pattern from left to right. Complete this row, then work rows 2 through 65 in the same manner.

chart 3

6 When all five pieces are completed, use available ends of warp and weft threads to carefully sew the four sides together, aligning the pieces row for row and passing through the outer beads of each piece. Sew one side of a chart 1 piece to one side of a chart 2 piece, the other side of this chart 2 piece to one side of the other chart 1 piece, etc. **(figures 1 and 2)**.

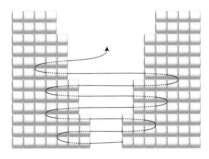

figure 1

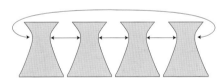

figure 2

7 Sew the edges of the chart 3 piece to the bottom of the vase.

8 Weave in all ends and clip threads close to the beadwork.

METAL SEED BEADS

Metal seed beads are irresistible, even though their surface finishes can be unstable. Some finishes wear off over time. Others have a metal lining that can be damaged by thread. Before you give in to temptation, learn about the different types so you can make the best choice for your project.

Precious metal beads are made from gold, silver, and gold and silver combined. To retain their luster, spray finished beadwork with clear acrylic glaze.

Silver-lined beads are made with crystal or other transparent glass. They contain a shiny silver lining that may rub off with too many thread passes. Handling the finished project will not affect the luster.

Galvanized beads are glass beads dipped in hot metal. They are attractive, but fragile and can dull while you're working. Toughen them up by pouring them into a plastic bag, spraying with a clear crystal glaze, and shaking them. Spray again when the beadwork is completed.

Luster, metallic, and metallic iris seed beads all have surface coatings that will rub off, so treat them with clear acrylic glaze.

24-karat gold–plated cut beads

silver-lined clear beads

galvanized silver beads

red-gold luster beads and metallic light bronze beads

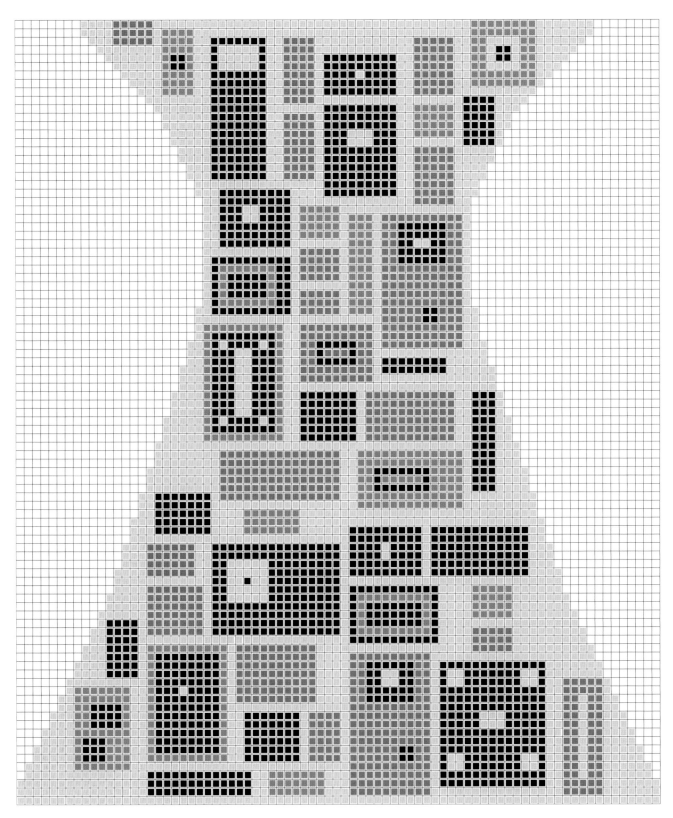

chart 1

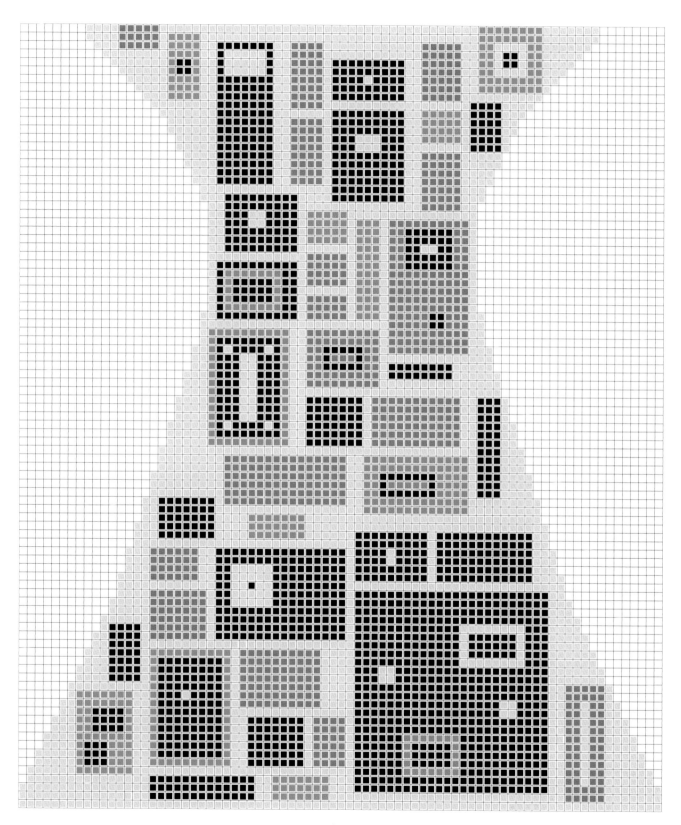

chart 2

Swan Handle Bracelet

Council Room Door

Bavarian by birth, Franz von Stuck spent the majority of his life in Munich, Germany, where he became a world-renowned illustrator, painter, sculptor, designer, and architect. In 1893 he was awarded a gold medal for his painting at the Chicago World's Fair. He received another at the 1900 Paris World Exposition for furniture design. Von Stuck built and designed everything for his home, Villa Stuck— from the architectural plans to the furniture and interior designs. While a professor at the Munich Academy, the artist taught notable students Josef Albers, Paul Klee, and Wassily Kandinsky. This door handle graces the entrance to the Council Room in Germany's Bremen City Hall.

(ERICH LESSING / ART RESOURCE, NY)

A RIOT OF FLORAL FORMS EMBELLISHES this door handle designed by Franz von Stuck. The artist's tangle of blooms is echoed in the frenetic wire spheres featured in this bracelet. Much as the wooden door offsets the metalwork, the wood beads in the bracelet offset the metal elements, and all the shapes and textures come together to form a harmonious whole.

FINISHED LENGTH:

8" (20.3 cm)

TECHNIQUES:

simple loop, wire spiral

MATERIALS AND TOOLS

- size 8° Czech seed beads (32), gold
- 3mm glass cubes (8), bronze
- 5 x 7mm rosewood saucers (16)
- 25mm mahogany vertically drilled flat square (1)
- 14 x 22mm antiqued brass leaf charm (1)
- 7mm antiqued brass jump rings (4)
- shiny brass eye pins (23)
- 26mm antiqued brass swan S clasp with 8mm rings (2)
- 24-gauge shiny brass wire (9 ½' [3 m])
- industrial-strength clear adhesive
- wire cutters
- round-nose pliers
- chain-nose pliers

1 String one seed bead, two saucers, and one seed bead on a head pin. Form a simple loop and trim any excess wire. Repeat to make eight wood bead links in all. Set aside.

2 String one seed bead, one cube, and one seed bead on a head pin. Form a simple loop and trim any excess wire. Repeat to make eight cube bead links in all. Set aside.

3 Cut one 18" (46 cm) piece of wire. Use round-nose pliers to make a loop at one end. Use the chain-nose pliers and your fingers to wrap the excess wire around the loop many times, much as you would a ball of yarn, to make an evenly shaped 10mm sphere as best you can.

Leave a ½" (1.5 cm) length of wire at the end and use chain-nose pliers to bend and tuck the wire into the body of the sphere. Pass an eye pin through the center of the sphere, making sure the eye pin's loop doesn't pull inside the tangled wires. Form a simple loop and trim any excess wire. Repeat to make six wire spheres in all. Set aside **(figure 1)**.

4 Pass an eye pin through the wood square bead. Form a simple loop and trim any excess wire. Set aside.

5 Cut a 3" (7.5 cm) piece of wire. Form a 4mm spiral at one end. Pass the other end through the leaf charm. Form another spiral at the other end. Repeat to add a second wire embellishment to the charm. Bend and arrange the spirals in a pleasing design. Glue the charm to the face of the wood square bead at a diagonal. Let the focal bead dry thoroughly **(figure 2)**.

figure 2

6 Connect one jump ring to a loop on the focal bead. Connect one cube link, one wire sphere, and one cube link. Attach each end of the chain to the jump ring **(figure 3)**.

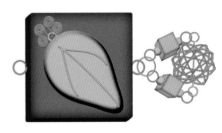

figure 3

figure 1

7 Connect one wood link, one sphere, and one wood link. Attach one end of the chain to one end of the first sphere, the other end to the other side of the same sphere. Repeat to add another wood link/sphere/wood link chain to the last sphere placed **(figure 4)**.

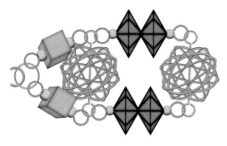

figure 4

8 Attach one cube link to each end of the last sphere. Use a jump ring to connect the two cube links. Attach one-half of the clasp to the jump ring.

9 Repeat steps 6 to 8 for the other side of the bracelet.

MAKING THE PERFECT LOOP

You'll have lots of practice with simple loops after making *Swan Handle Bracelet*, but you'll want to know how to make perfect loops before you begin.

1. After stringing your beads, cut the wire to ⅜" (1 cm) from the bead hole. Use chain-nose pliers to grasp the end of the wire and make a right angle.

2. Use round-nose pliers to grasp the very tip of the wire. Turn your wrist completely over. The loop is complete once the wire tip touches the bend.

3. Use round- and chain-nose pliers to adjust the loop so it is flat and centered over the beads. The loop should look like an **O,** not a **P.**

Laburnum Bracelet

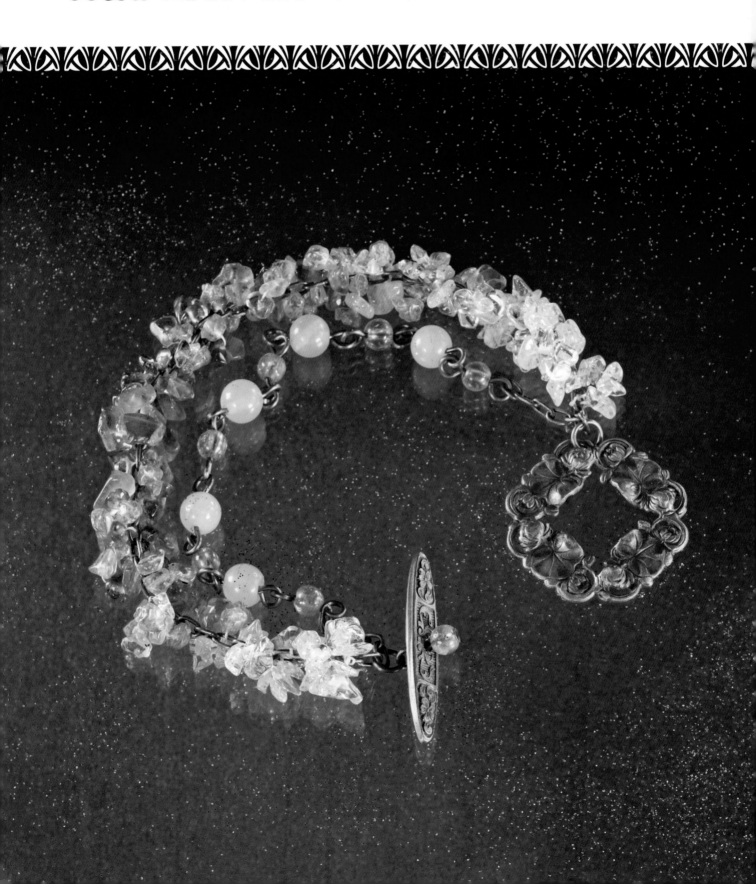

Laburnum Lamp

Louis Comfort Tiffany was the premier American artist in the Art Nouveau movement. His father, Charles Lewis Tiffany, was founder of the famous Tiffany & Company jewelry store. Louis Tiffany was known primarily for his ornate stained-glass lamps and windows. Stylized floral forms were his signature subjects, and his glasswork often featured a wide array of colored opalescent and sometimes imperfect blown glass. Tiffany started his career as a painter, working in New York, Paris, and Morocco, but later opened an interior design firm where he created stained glass, pottery, jewelry, and other objets d'art. This Laburnum lamp is in a private collection.

(ART RESOURCE, NY)

GLISTENING SEMIPRECIOUS STONES mimic the rich and luminescent colors in this Tiffany lamp, which features sweeping laburnum leaves. Brass chain and an Art Nouveau–inspired clasp provide a functional and unifying metallic accent. Wear the bracelet twisted for a tight ropelike effect or let the chains loosely separate for a more freeform style.

FINISHED LENGTH:

7½" (19 cm)

TECHNIQUES:

simple loop, sewing, opening and closing rings

MATERIALS AND TOOLS

· 4mm semiprecious iolite saucers (18)

· 4mm semiprecious peridot rounds (7)

· 5mm semiprecious citrine chips (72)

· 5mm semiprecious peridot chips (64)

· 5mm semiprecious amethyst chips (32)

· 6mm semiprecious yellow jade rounds (5)

· 5mm antiqued brass jump rings (2)

· antiqued brass eye pins (11), 1" (2.5 cm)

· antiqued brass head pin (1), 1½" (4 cm)

· 25mm antiqued brass square filigree ring with floral design (1)

· 30mm antiqued brass toggle bar (1)

· 2 x 4mm antiqued copper chain, 7¾" (19.5 cm)

· 6-lb. test braided beading thread, white

· size 12 beading needle

· scissors

· chain-nose pliers

· round-nose pliers

· wire cutters

1 String one peridot bead on the head pin and pass the pin through the toggle bar from front to back. Form a simple loop to secure the bead. Set aside **(figure 1)**.

figure 1

2 String one peridot bead on an eye pin and form a simple loop to secure the bead **(figure 2)**. Repeat to make six peridot links in all. Set aside.

figure 2

3 String one jade bead on an eye pin and form a simple loop to secure the bead. Repeat to make five jade links in all. Set aside.

4 Make a chain using alternating peridot and jade links. Set aside.

5 Thread the needle with approximately 3' (1 m) of thread. Use a strong knot to tie the thread to a link about 1" (2.5 cm) from the end of the copper chain. Pick up four citrine chips and pass down through the next link on the chain. Repeat down the chain, adding half of the citrine chips **(figure 3)**. Make knots on the chain every few stitches to secure the stones.

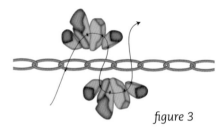

figure 3

Continue to add chips, blending from citrine to peridot, peridot to iolite, iolite to amethyst, and back again, leaving 1" (2.5 cm) of bare chain at each end. Tie a strong knot to the last link stitched and trim the thread.

6 Connect one jump ring to the copper link that sits in front of the stitched section. Before you close the ring, attach the toggle bar **(figure 4)**.

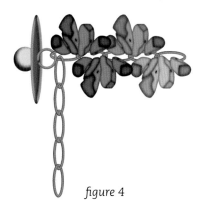

figure 4

7 Repeat at the other end of the stitched section, adding the toggle bar.

8 Connect each end of the copper chain to the ends of the bead link chain.

ALTERING BRASS FINISHES

It's easy to alter the look of brass findings like the clasp in *Laburnum Bracelet*. In this project, the purchased clasp had an antiqued finish, but a few strokes of fine-grit sandpaper gave it a shiny finish, making it look more like the Tiffany lamp parts in the inspiration photo on page 37.

To darken brass, you can simply heat it over an open flame. Heating the brass also removes any factory finishes or sealers, allowing oxidization to occur.

Another way to alter a brass finish is with spray paint. First, heat the finding over a flame and let it cool. Spray two or more very light coats of enamel paint on each side of the finding, allowing the paint to dry thoroughly between coats. Give the brass a final coat of clear enamel to seal the new finish.

Lalique Earrings

Lalique Perfume Bottle

René Jules Lalique was one of Art Nouveau's most prolific jewelers and glassworkers. Born in Ay, France, in 1860, he apprenticed with a Parisian jeweler before attending Sydenham Art College in London, England. In 1885, after a short freelance career designing for other French jewelers, he opened his own jewelry workshop. Five years later, he was an established designer of the Art Nouveau movement, creating pieces for La Maison de l'Art Nouveau in Paris. He made this glass perfume bottle with gold mount between 1902 and 1905. It is in the Musée d'Orsay in Paris.

(*Réunion des Musées Nationaux / Art Resource, NY*)

TO MIMIC THE GOLD MOUNT on this Lalique perfume bottle, these earrings have swirls of gold seed beads sewn to a filigreed bead cap, which is then topped with a golden crystal. Faceted crystal drops reference the glass bottle, adding a bit of sparkle to the earrings, too.

FINISHED LENGTH:

1³⁄₈" (3.5 cm) long, plus ear wire

TECHNIQUES:

simple loops

MATERIALS AND TOOLS

· size 15° seed beads, 1 g 24-karat gold–plated

· size 11° seed beads, 1 g 24-karat gold–plated

· 20 x 12mm clear rock crystal faceted teardrops (2)

· 9 x 10mm filigreed vermeil bead caps (2)

· 4mm bicone crystals: (2) crystal, (2) gold colored

· 2" (5 cm) gold-plated head pins (2)

· gold-filled French ear wires (2)

· 6-lb. test braided beading thread

· size 12 beading needle

· scissors

· wire cutters

· round-nose pliers

· chain-nose pliers

1 Thread a needle with 12" (30.5 cm) of thread and anchor it to the bottom row of the filigree on a bead cap. With the thread in front of the cap, *pick up one 11° seed bead and four 15° seed beads. Pass from front to back through a higher row of filigree, slightly to the left of the starting place, forming a slanted row of seed beads **(figure 1)**.

figure 1

2 With the thread exiting the space to the left of the starting place, repeat from * of step 1. Repeat this around the bead cap. The number of strands may vary, depending on the pattern of your bead cap. The example shows nine slanted strands. Secure the thread and trim.

3 Use a head pin to pick up one crystal bicone, one rock crystal teardrop, the beaded bead cap from inside to outside, one 11° seed bead, and one gold bicone **(figure 2)**.

4 With your fingers, bend the headpin over the top of the last bead forming a right angle. Form a simple loop to secure the beads **(figure 3)**.

figure 3

5 Open the loop on the ear wire and slide the dangle onto the loop. Close the loop.

Repeat steps 1 through 5 to make a second earring.

GOLDEN EAR-WIRE OPTIONS

There are several options when it comes to ear wires, depending on what you're hanging. Our choice for dressy earrings like the *Lalique Earrings* is plain gold-filled French wires, as shown below, far left. Other available styles, shown from left to right, include French wires with a bead and coil, lever-back ear wires, ear strings, and hoops.

In addition to various styles, "gold" ear findings also come in different materials: 14-karat gold, gold-filled, vermeil, and gold plated.

- 14-karat gold is a little more than 50 percent pure gold mixed with other metals to make it hard enough to use for jewelry components.

- Gold-filled wires have a solid layer of gold bonded to a base of brass or other metal. Gold-filled items are long lasting and look almost as good as pure gold.

- Vermeil is gold in color but is a combination of precious metals, most commonly sterling silver coated with 14-karat gold. Vermeil is usually used for decorative findings.

- Gold-plated wires are inexpensive, an acceptable choice for casual or "fun" earrings. A thin layer of gold is deposited over copper or silver through an electrochemical process. This thin layer rubs off rather quickly, so if you wear your earrings often, they will eventually turn silver or copper.

plain gold-filled French wire   *French wire with a bead and coil*   *lever-back ear wire*   *ear string*   *hoop*

Chat Noir Bracelet

Chat Noir Poster

Théophile Alexandre Steinlen was born in Lausanne, Switzerland, in 1859, and made his way to eastern France where he worked in a textile mill. He and his wife moved to the Montmartre quarter in Paris, where he found an active and supportive artistic community. Primarily known for his posters, such as those for the Chat Noir, a Paris nightclub, Steinlen was also a prolific painter. He created hundreds of lithographs and illustrations and even dabbled in sculpture. Well known for his love of animals, which appeared in many of his works, Steinlen also gained fame for his renderings of everyday life in Montmartre, often exposing the darker side of society.

(GIRAUDON / ART RESOURCE, NY)

PRINT, BEADS, AND PERIOD-INSPIRED filigree combine in homage to the lively Paris cabaret scene of the 1890s. This project incorporates a variety of techniques, including collage, bead embroidery, tubular peyote stitch, patina, and even a little metalwork. Although the days of the cabaret are over, wearing this piece just might transport you to the smoky sensuality and lively drama of the times.

FINISHED LENGTH:

7 ½" (19 cm)

TECHNIQUES:

collage, bead embroidery, tubular peyote stitch, patina, opening and closing rings

MATERIALS AND TOOLS

- size 15° seed beads, 2 g black
- size 11° seed beads, 2 g burgundy
- size 9° seed beads, 10 g red
- 20mm vertically drilled flat square shell beads (4), white
- 12 x 30mm brass filigree bars (6)
- 15 x 20mm brass filigree butterflies (4)
- 12 x 15mm sterling silver square box clasp with filigree design (1)
- 4.5mm antiqued brass jump rings (18)
- 6-lb. test braided beading thread, black
- stiff felt, black (6" [15 cm] square)
- Ultrasuede, black (6" [15 cm] square)
- paper printed with images and words, red and black on white
- rubber stamps, French text and starburst
- permanent stamping ink, black
- permanent markers, black and red
- adhesive glaze, clear
- glue stick, clear
- adhesive cement, clear
- cardboard box or newspaper
- spray enamel, black and clear
- liver of sulfur
- sandpaper
- small paintbrush
- scissors
- size 12 beading needle
- chain-nose pliers
- gas stove or torch
- fireproof tongs
- ceramic dish
- plastic container for liver of sulfur
- copper tongs

MAKING THE CABOCHONS

1 Lightly sand each shell square to remove any polish and roughen the surface. Set aside.

2 Use the printed paper, rubber stamps, markers, and glue stick to create a collage small enough to fit on a shell bead (page 49). Let dry. Repeat to make four unique collages in all.

3 Brush a light coat of glaze onto one of the shells. Layer the collage onto the shell. Let dry. Brush two or more coats on top of the collage, allowing the glaze to dry thoroughly between coats. If the collage hangs over the shell's edge, use scissors to carefully trim away any excess. Repeat for the remaining collages. Set the cabochons aside (**figure 1**).

figure 1

4 Cut the felt into four 1½" (4 cm) squares. Use adhesive cement to glue one cabochon (face up) to the center of each of the felt squares. Let dry.

MAKING THE BEZELS

5 Thread the needle with approximately 3' (1 m) of thread. Tie a knot at one end. Pass through the felt from back to front, exiting right next to the cabochon.

ROUND 1: Pick up two 9° beads, lay them along the edge of the cabochon, and pass down through the felt right next to the second bead. Pass up through the felt between the first and second beads and pass through the second bead, making a back stitch **(figure 2)**.

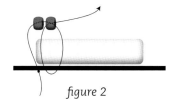

figure 2

Repeat around the cabochon to make a bead-embroidered ring that edges the cabochon. Make sure that the ring has an even number of beads.

ROUND 2: Use 9° beads to work tubular peyote stitch off the first round **(figure 3)**.

figure 3

ROUNDS 3 AND 4: Use 9° beads to work two more rounds of tubular peyote stitch.

ROUND 5: Work the round using 11° beads. Pull tight so the beadwork slightly cups over the cabochon. Secure the thread and trim.

6 Trim the felt close to the cabochon, taking care to not snip any stitches.

7 Trace the cabochon on the Ultrasuede and cut out the shape. Use adhesive to glue the suede to the back of the felt. Let dry.

8 Start a new thread that exits from a round 1 bead. Use 9° beads to work two rounds of tubular peyote stitch off of round 1 **(figure 4)**.

figure 4

9 Use 11° beads to work two more rounds of tubular peyote stitch. Pull tightly to allow the beadwork to cup the cabochon. Use 15° beads to work two final rounds, pulling very tightly so the beadwork lays flat on the back of the cabochon. Secure the thread and trim.

10 Start a new thread that exits from a round 1 corner bead. Pick up seven 15° beads and pass through the corner bead again to make a loop. Weave through the round 1 beads to the next corner and make another seven-bead loop. Repeat for the remaining two corners **(figure 5)**.

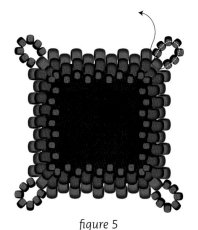

figure 5

11 Repeat steps 5 through 10 for each cabochon. Set aside.

REFINISHING THE FILIGREE

12 Working in a well-ventilated area, turn on the stove or torch. Use fireproof tongs to grasp one of the filigree pieces and place it in the flame until red hot. This removes any finishing from the brass. Place the filigree on the ceramic dish and let cool. Repeat for all the filigree pieces.

13 Working in a well-ventilated area, place all the filigree pieces in the box or on the newspaper. Use the black enamel to lightly coat the pieces. Let dry. Turn over and spray another coat. Let dry for several hours. Turn the pieces to the front and spray a clear coat. Let dry for twenty-four hours. Set aside.

14 Working in a well-ventilated area, prepare the liver of sulfur in the plastic container according to the manufacturer's directions. Use copper tongs to dip the clasp in the solution until black. Rinse with water and set aside.

ASSEMBLY

15 Pair two filigree butterflies back to back. Place one jump ring at the upper corners to attach the pieces together. Before closing, connect each ring to a loop on one side of a cabochon. At the bottom of the butterfly, use one jump ring to connect one-half of the clasp (**figure 6**).

figure 6

16 Pair two filigree bars back to back. Place one jump ring at each corner to attach the pieces together. Before closing, connect two rings to the loops on the other side of the cabochon attached to the butterfly. Connect the other two rings to two loops on a second cabochon (**figure 7**).

figure 7

17 Use jump rings and bars to connect the rest of the cabochons.

18 Repeat step 15 to attach the remaining butterfly pieces and the other half of the clasp.

COLLAGE BEADS

Adding images to beads is a fun way to personalize your jewelry-making projects. The collages in *Chat Noir Bracelet* were done like mini artworks—the sanded shell beads are a perfect canvas. Like any artist, You can choose from an endless variety of materials—your imagination is the only limit! Here are the items used for the collages in the bracelet on page 44.

Scans. The large blocks of color are details from antique wallpaper that was scanned and printed with the computer. Favorite portions of the color pattern were then trimmed out using tiny scissors.

Print. The font feature on your computer's word-processing program is a great tool. There are several typefaces on the inspiration poster on page 45, so it was easy to find similar styles. You can also change the font color to add another design element.

Rubber stamps. Rubber stamps lightly coated with permanent stamping inks were used to decorate the collage. The stamps in these tiny collages sometime sit in the foreground and other times are hidden behind print and scans. By mixing up the positioning, you'll give your collage depth.

Markers. You can fill in color gaps or create new images with bold permanent markers with various tip weights.

Adhesive glaze. This glaze is the glue that holds everything together. Get a good-quality glaze that dries clear. Also make sure to let each layer of glaze dry thoroughly between coats.

Galeries Lafayette Dome Pendant

Galeries Lafayette Dome

An elaborate skylight in the Galeries Lafayette department store in Paris is a fine example of Art Nouveau's presence in everyday life—everything in sight was a potential work of art. In 1912, owner Théophile Bader commissioned architects Georges Chedanne and Ferdinand Chanut to design the layout for the new store. Flooding the main hall with golden light, the glass and steel dome is the centerpiece of the building, which also features Art Nouveau staircases.

(Archive Timothy McCarthy / Art Resource, NY)

THIS SKYLIGHT DOME just looked like a pendant waiting to be strung for a necklace! The opalescence of the milky white glass is achieved with a mother-of-pearl donut, and the crystal disk in the center lets the light through when the pendant is hung in a window. The spiral stitch cord may be lengthened or shortened to suit your personal style.

FINISHED LENGTH:

17" (43 cm) cord (including clasp),
2" (50 mm) pendant

TECHNIQUES:

square stitch, peyote stitch,
picots, spiral stitch

MATERIALS AND TOOLS

- size 15° seed beads: 5 g silver-lined
  dark topaz, 5 g metallic silver, 1 g
  silver-lined sapphire

- size 11° cylinder beads: 2 g silver-lined
  dark topaz, 3 g silver-lined sapphire

- 50mm mother-of-pearl donut with
  10mm center hole (1)

- 10mm crystal disk (1), dark blue

- silver hook-and-eye clasp (1)

- size D nylon beading thread

- wax or thread conditioner

- size 12 and 13 beading needles

- scissors

Note: Use the size 13 needle if the
beads get too filled with thread to
pass a size 12 needle through.

MAKING THE SQUARE-STITCHED STRIPS

1 Thread a size 12 needle with 3'
(1 m) of thread and wax well. Make a
twenty-five-row strip of three-bead-
wide square stitch as follows:

Row 1: three 15° topaz beads.
Row 2: one 15° topaz bead, one 15°
silver bead, one 15° topaz bead.

Repeat rows 1 and 2 eleven more
times, then repeat row 1 one more
time **(figure 1)**.

figure 1

2 To begin the second strip, pick
up one topaz cylinder bead and three
15° topaz beads, then begin to work
another twenty-five-row strip of
three-bead-wide square stitch as
outlined in step 1. Be sure to work
with tight tension **(figure 2)**.

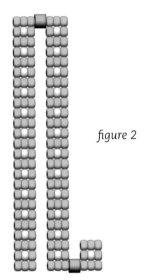

figure 2

3 Repeat steps 1 and 2 until you
have nine three-bead-wide strips
(figure 3).

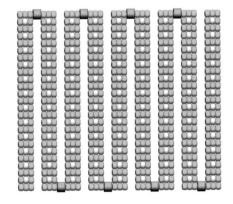

figure 3

ATTACHING THE STRIPS
TO THE DONUT

4 Each strip is folded in half around the donut and the ends are joined by passing the thread through the center hole of the donut. Beginning with the first strip, fold the strip in half around the donut so the ends of the strip align with the center edge of the donut. With the thread exiting an outside bead in the row second from the end, pass through the first row of the strip in one direction, through the center hole of the donut to the other side, then through the last row in the opposite direction **(figure 4)**.

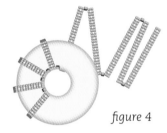

figure 4

5 Pass through the cylinder bead and the first three beads of the next strip. Fold this strip in half around the donut and join the ends at the center hole as outlined in step 4 **(figure 5)**.

figure 5

Continue in this manner, adding a cylinder bead as necessary, first on the front, then on the back of the donut, until you have nine strips encasing the donut.

6 On the outside edge of the donut, pick up ten topaz cylinder beads between each strip, passing through the three beads of the center row (row 13) of each strip **(figure 6)**.

figure 6

7 Work one round of peyote stitch off the ten beads between each strip with topaz cylinder beads, passing again through the center row of each strip when necessary, forming three rounds of peyote stitch **(figure 7)**.

figure 7

8 Work two rounds of peyote stitch on the front with 15° topaz beads. Work one round of peyote stitch on the front with 15° silver beads **(figure 8)**. Work two rounds of peyote stitch on the back with 15° topaz beads.

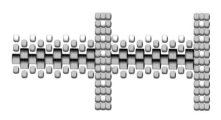

figure 8

MAKING THE CENTER
OF THE PENDANT

9 Attach a thread to the beads at the inside of the pendant. Pick up the 10mm disk and pass through a few beads at the opposite side of the center hole. Weave back through the work to exit from the first bead you passed through on this side of the hole, and pass through the crystal disk again **(figure 9)**.

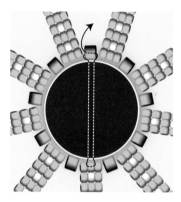

figure 9

Pass through these beads and the disk several times to reinforce.

10 With the thread exiting the next cylinder bead between two strips, *pick up three 15° silver beads and pass through the next cylinder bead. Repeat from * around the disk (**figure 10**).

figure 10

11 Pass through the first three 15° silver beads added in step 10. *Pick up one 15° silver bead, one 15° sapphire bead, and one 15° silver bead, then pass through the next three 15° silver beads added in step 10, forming a picot. Repeat from * around the inside of the pendant (**figure 11**).

figure 11

12 With the thread exiting the center sapphire bead of the next picot formed in step 11, *pick up one topaz cylinder bead and pass through the sapphire bead in the center of the next picot. Repeat from * around (**figure 12**).

figure 12

Pass through all beads of this round again.

13 Pull the thread of this last round very tightly, forming a cup over the edges of the disk. Secure the thread well, but don't trim.

14 Weave through the work and add one sapphire cylinder bead between each strip around the center of the pendant, passing through the second row of each strip (**figure 13**).

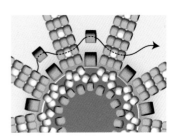

figure 13

EMBELLISHING THE PENDANT

15 With thread exiting the ninth row on the front of a strip, *pick up one silver 15° bead, one sapphire 15° bead, and one silver 15° bead. Pass through the next (tenth) row, forming a picot. Repeat from * on the other side, passing through the ninth row to form the picot (**figure 14**).

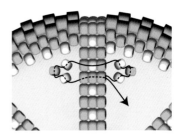

figure 14

16 Weave through the beadwork to add picots to both sides of each strip as outlined in step 15.

MAKING THE BAIL

17 Using topaz cylinder beads and working off the front row of cylinders in the outer peyote rounds, make a four-bead-wide peyote strip centered between two strips. Make the strip twenty rows long (count ten beads along each side of the strip) **(figure 15)**.

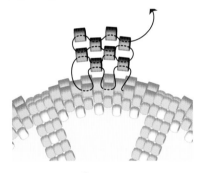

figure 15

18 Embellish the edges of the bail by adding picots of one silver 15° bead, one sapphire 15° bead, and one silver 15° bead along both edges of the strip **(figure 16)**.

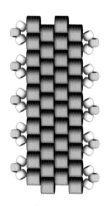

figure 16

19 Sew the last row of the bail to the third row of cylinders in the outer peyote-stitched rounds (figure 17) Secure all threads and trim.

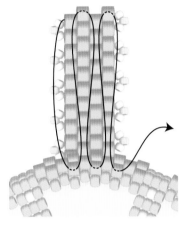

figure 17

MAKING THE SPIRAL CORD

20 Make a cord of regular spiral stitch, using four sapphire cylinder beads as the core and five 15° beads as the outer beads as follows: silver, topaz, silver, topaz, silver. Continue until the cord is 16" (41 cm) or desired length **(figure 18)**.

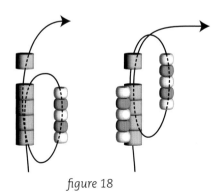

figure 18

FINISHING

21 Slide the bail over the cord.

22 Attach the hook part of the clasp to one end of the cord and the eye end to the other by passing through the end of the cord, stringing eight silver 15° beads, passing through the clasp half, and passing again through the end of the cord **(figure 19)**.

figure 19

Reinforce the connection by passing through all beads several more times.

23 Secure all threads and trim.

Scheherazade Necklace

Set design for Scheherazade

Léon Bakst was born Lev Rosenberg in 1866 in what is now called Belarus. He was at the forefront of the Russian Art Nouveau movement, or *Mir Iskusstva* (World of Art). The primary head of the movement was Sergei Diaghilev, who, with Bakst, started an influential magazine of the same name. In fact, Bakst's illustrations and paintings became famous from his work with the magazine. Bakst taught painting most of his life, moving back and forth between St. Petersburg and Paris. Toward the end of his life, he primarily created set designs for Diaghilev's Ballets Russes, such as this one for the *Scheherazade*.

(GIRAUDON / ART RESOURCE, NY)

MODELED AFTER THE SUMPTUOUS DÉCOR in the harem room for the ballet *Scheherazade*, this sparkling crystal-link pendant in jewel tones evokes the exotic and erotic. Once stitched together, the necklace's chain and sparkling beads create the image of a lantern as it casts its glow on 1,001 tales.

FINISHED LENGTH:

25" (63.5 cm) neckline,
4" (10 cm) pendant

TECHNIQUES:

tubular peyote stitch, peyote stitch
decreases, simple fringe, picots,
simple loop, wrapped loop, opening
and closing rings

MATERIALS AND TOOLS

- size 10° Czech seed beads,
  5 g translucent light pink

- size 15° Japanese seed beads,
  5 g silver-lined red

- 4mm crystal bicones (21), peridot

- 4mm crystal bicones (128),
  smoky topaz

- 6mm crystal rounds (4), ruby red

- 8mm crystal rounds (6), ruby red

- 16 x 21mm resin round (1),
  translucent light gray

- 4 x 6mm gold oval jump rings (32)

- 7mm gold round jump ring (1)

- 22-gauge gold-filled head pins,
  2" (5 cm) (6)

- 6 x 8mm shiny brass decorative chain
  (27" [68.5 cm])

- 22-gauge shiny brass wire (5½" [14 cm])

- acrylic floor wax (optional)

- 6-lb. test braided beading thread

- scissors

- size 12 beading needle

- wire cutters and round-nose pliers

- one pair of round-nose pliers and
  two pairs of chain-nose pliers

1 Thread the needle with approximately 6' (2 m) of thread. Leaving a 4" (10 cm) tail, pick up enough 10° beads to fit around the widest circumference of the resin bead. Make sure you've chosen an even number of beads. Tie a square knot to make a circle and slide it on the resin bead (**figure 1**).

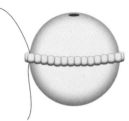

figure 1

2 Use 10° beads to work several rounds of tubular peyote stitch off the initial circle. Once the resin bead begins to curve, keep the beadwork in place as you make enough decreases in each round to keep the beadwork close to the resin bead. The decreases don't have to be perfectly spaced because they won't be seen. Just keep the beadwork centered around the bead hole.

Once you reach the hole, weave through the last-round beads several times, making sure to leave a small opening for a head pin. Weave through the beadwork to exit from a first-round bead. Repeat to bead the bottom half of the resin bead, this time beginning with a few rows of 10° beads, and then using 15° beads only once you start making decreases. Secure the thread and trim.

3 Start a new thread that exits from a 15° bead about seven rounds from the bead hole. *Pick up one topaz bicone and one 15° bead. Pass back through the bicone and into the next 15° bead in the round. Skip one 15° bead in the round and weave through the beads to exit from the next one. Repeat from * around the beaded bead to make a circle of fringe legs centered around the beaded bead's hole (**figure 2**). Exit from a 15° bead at the end of one of the legs.

figure 2

4 Pick up one topaz bicone and pass through the 15° bead at the end of the next fringe leg. Repeat around to connect all the fringes into a circle (**figure 3**). Weave through all several times to reinforce. Weave through the beads to exit from a 15° bead added in the first decrease round of the beaded bead.

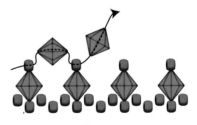

figure 3

5 Pick up one topaz bicone and one 15° bead. Pass back through the bicone and into the next 15° bead in the round. Repeat around to add one fringe leg between each bead of the round. The legs will sit diagonally to the fringes added in step 3. Weave through the beads to exit from a 10° bead three rounds down on the beaded bead from where you placed the last fringe legs, and repeat the step to add one fringe leg between each bead of the round. Exit from a 15° bead added in this step.

6 Pick up two 15° beads and pass through the 15° bead of the fringe leg that's diagonally placed on the previous row of fringe legs. Pick up one peridot bicone and pass through the 15° bead of the next fringe leg on the previous round. Repeat around to connect the two rounds of fringe **(figure 4)**.

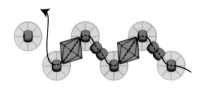

figure 4

7 Weave through the beads to exit from a 10° bead two rounds down on the beaded bead from where you placed the last fringe. Pick up one 15° bead and pass through the next bead in the round to "stitch in the ditch." Repeat around the beaded bead. Exit through a bead added in this step.

8 Pick up one 15° bead, one topaz bicone, and one 15° bead. Pass back through the bicone and pick up one 15° bead. Pass through the next 15° bead added in the previous step **(figure 5)**. Repeat to add picots around the beaded bead. Exit from the 15° bead at the top of one of the picots.

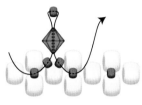

figure 5

9 Pick up one topaz bicone and pass through the 15° bead at the top of the next picot, as in step 4. Repeat around to connect the picots. Pass through all the beads again to reinforce. Exit from a bicone.

10 Pick up one 15° bead, one topaz bicone, and one 15° bead. Pass back through the bicone and pick up one 15° bead. Pass through the next bicone added in the previous step. Repeat to add a second round of picots. Exit from the 15° bead at the top of one of the picots **(figure 6)**.

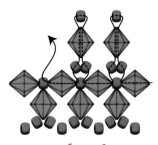

figure 6

11 Pick up two 15° beads and pass through the 15° bead at the top of the next picot. Repeat around to connect all the picots, forming a ring. Pass through all the beads again to reinforce. Secure the thread and trim. If desired, dip the beaded bead in floor wax and let dry to strengthen.

12 Attach one oval jump ring to a point on the 15° bead ring created in the previous step. Repeat around to place a total of four to eight oval jump rings equidistant apart.

Note: The number of jump rings you use will determine how many small chains you'll need to connect the beaded bead to the decorative chain necklace. Set the beaded bead aside.

13 Take apart the decorative chain to make one 20" (51 cm), one 3½" (9 cm), and one 3" (7.5 cm) length. Set aside.

14 Connect the remaining oval jump rings to make four to eight three-link chains. Set aside.

15 Cut three 1" (2.5 cm) pieces of wire. Form a simple loop at one end of one wire. Slip on an 8mm round and form another simple loop to secure the bead. Repeat for the other wires. Set the large bead links aside.

16 Cut one ¾" (2 cm) piece of wire. Form a simple loop at one end. Slip on a 6mm round and form another simple loop to secure the bead. Set the small bead link aside.

17 Check that the 3½" (9 cm) chain has an odd number of links. If not, remove one. Add the small bead link to the center link of this chain. Add a large bead link to the small link.

18 Use one large bead link to connect the end of the 20" (51 cm) chain to one end of the 3½" (9 cm) chain. Repeat for the other chain ends. Set the necklace aside.

Opening Jump Rings

It's tempting to be lazy and open jump rings with just one set of chain-nose pliers and your fingers, but it's best to use two sets to keep your jump rings flat and even, giving the most professional-looking results. Using two pliers also keeps your closures tighter and neater, especially with heavy decorative rings (and will definitely save you a trip to the manicurist).

19 Take apart the 3" (7.5 cm) chain to make one eight-link, two two-link, and three one-link pieces. Slide an 8mm round on a head pin. Begin a wrapped loop, but before making the wrap, slide the loop onto an end link of the eight-link chain (**figure 7**). Make the wrap to secure the dangle.

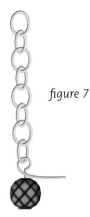

figure 7

Repeat, using the remaining rounds and head pins to make one dangle for each of the remaining links. Randomly connect the small embellished links to the eight-link chain to make a pleasing chain fringe (**figure 8**).

figure 8

20 Cut a 1¾" (4.5 cm) length of wire. Form a wide simple loop at one end of the wire and attach the open end of the chain fringe. Pass the wire through the beaded bead and form another simple loop to secure the bead. Attach the large bead link at the end of the chain necklace to the loop.

21 Connect one of the three-link jump ring chains from step 14 to an oval jump ring attached to the beaded bead. Repeat around to add all the jump-ring chains. Open the round jump ring and slide on the end link of each jump-ring chain in order. Before closing, lay the connected bead links within the ring (**figure 9**).

figure 9

CHAIN OPTIONS

The purchased chain used for this project is clean and sleek, allowing the pendant to take center stage. If you prefer to make a beaded chain, here are a few options.

The *first variation* shown here employs a simple stringing technique with 6mm ruby bicone crystals, 3mm golden shadow crystals, and 8° and 11° 24-karat gold–plated seed beads. With two strands of beading wire exiting an 11° seed bead, *string one 8° seed bead and one 3mm crystal three times followed by one 8° seed bead on each strand. Pass both strands through one 11° seed bead, one 6mm crystal, and one 11° seed bead. Repeat from * to desired length.

The *second variation* is made of spiral stitch with 11° ruby and 11° 24-karat gold–plated seed beads. Follow the instructions on page 90 for spiral stitch, using four ruby beads for the core and three gold beads for the outer beads.

The *third variation* is made with a simple daisy chain of 11° ruby and 11° 24-karat gold–plated seed beads. String eight gold beads and form a circle by passing through the first bead strung. Pick up one ruby bead and pass through the gold bead opposite the first bead (this will be the fifth bead strung). *Pick up one gold bead and pass

variation 1

variation 2

variation 3

through the next bead on the circle (the sixth bead strung). Pick up one gold bead and pass back through the last bead just added. Pick up six gold beads and pass through the second bead added in this step. Pick up one ruby bead and pass through the bead opposite the bead just exited. Repeat from * to desired length.

Nouveau Tilework Necklace

Nouveau Tilework Tub

France's two main centers for Art Nouveau were Paris and Nancy, but the art form was evident in the architecture and decoration in many towns. This elaborate Art Nouveau bathtub is part of the thermal baths of Aix-les-Bains, France. Celtic horsemen discovered the hot spring waters in this area, and formal baths were first built in 1784. Many renovations and expansions have since taken place, including those of the early twentieth century, which included the addition of this tub.

(*Erich Lessing / Art Resource, NY*)

THE INSPIRATION FOR THIS NECKLACE is a magnificent tiled bathtub that is part of the Thermal Baths at Aix-les-Bains, France. The amazonite stones used in the necklace closely resemble the tiles, and the gold accents mimic the stripes between the tiles. Some artistic license was taken to include the black crystals, but the black complements the green and gold, and the crystal adds sparkle.

FINISHED LENGTH:

18" (45.5 cm)

TECHNIQUES:

stringing, wirework

MATERIALS AND TOOLS

· 18 x 24mm amazonite pillow
  beads (4)

· 10mm round amazonite beads (3)

· 6mm round amazonite beads (36)

· 3mm round amazonite beads (38)

· 4mm crystal bicones (98), jet black

· size 11° hex-cut seed beads (172),
  24-karat gold–plated

· size 15° seed beads (288),
  metallic gold

· 5mm thin gold daisy spacers (20)

· 15mm vermeil three-strand
  connector (4)

· 15mm vermeil three-strand reducer (2)

· vermeil hook-and-eye clasp (1)

· 2mm gold jump rings (2)

· 20-gauge gold-filled half-hard wire,
  8" (20.5 cm)

· 6-lb. test braided beading thread

· size 12 beading needle

· scissors

· wire cutters

· round-nose pliers

· chain-nose pliers

MAKING THE CENTERPIECE

1 Straighten the 8" (20.5 cm) of wire in your fingers and cut it in half with the wire cutters. Form a small simple loop at one end of each piece. Pick up the following sequence of beads onto each wire: one spacer, one bicone, one hex bead, one 3mm round, one hex bead, one bicone, one spacer, one pillow bead, one spacer, one bicone, one spacer, one pillow bead, one spacer, one bicone, and one spacer.

Bend the end of the wire at a 90-degree angle and make a small simple loop that finishes flush to the last spacer **(figure 1)**. Set aside. Repeat to make a second pendant.

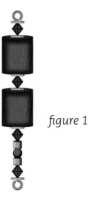

figure 1

2 Thread a needle with 24" (61 cm) of thread. Pick up one daisy spacer, one bicone, one spacer, and fourteen 15° beads. Leaving a 3" (7.5 cm) tail, pass through the inside hole of a three-strand connector, forming a loop of seed beads through the hole, and back through the spacer, bicone, and spacer. Pull taut and knot the thread ends **(figure 2)**.

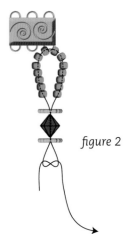

figure 2

3 *Pick up one 10mm round, one spacer, one bicone, one pendant, one bicone, and one spacer. Repeat from * one more time. String one 10mm round, one spacer, one bicone, one spacer, and fourteen 15° beads. Pass through the inside hole of a second three-strand connector, forming a loop of seed beads through the hole **(figure 3)**.

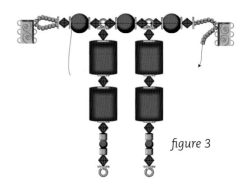

figure 3

f the holes in your connector or reducer are too small to allow 15° beads to pass through, pick up half the required beads, pass through the hole, then thread the other half of the beads **(figure 4)**.

figure 4

Skip the last seed beads strung and pass back through the rest of the beads just strung until you reach the first spacer on the opposite side. Pull the thread taut.

4 *Pick up sixteen 15° beads and pass through the middle hole of the three-strand connector on this end, forming a loop of seed beads through the hole. Pass back through the previously strung beads to the other side and repeat from * **(figure 5)**.

figure 5

5 *Pick up eighteen 15° beads and pass through the outside hole of the three-strand connector on this end, forming a loop of seed beads through the hole. Pass back through the previously strung beads to the other side and repeat from *.

6 Pass back through one spacer, one bicone, one spacer, and one 10mm round. Tie the working thread around the thread between the 10mm round and the spacer, using a half-hitch knot **(figure 6)**.

figure 6

Weave back through the beads to further reinforce the centerpiece, making a knot at the other side. Pull the thread taut and trim. Set aside.

MAKING THE SIDE SECTIONS

7 Thread a needle with approximately 18" (45.5 cm) of thread. Pick up one 6mm round, one hex bead, one bicone, and eight 15° beads. Leaving a 3" (7.5 cm) tail, pass through the inside hole of one of the three-strand connectors attached to the centerpiece, forming a loop of seed beads through this hole. Pass back through the bicone, hex bead, and 6mm round. Pull the threads taut and tie them together with an overhand knot **(figure 7)**.

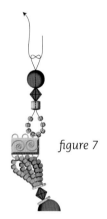

figure 7

8 *Pick up one hex bead, one bicone, one hex bead, and one 6mm round; repeat from * four more times. Pick up one hex bead, one bicone, and eight 15° beads. Pass through the inside hole of a new three-strand connector, forming a loop of seed beads through this hole. Pass back through all beads between the two connectors a couple of times. Tie the working thread around the thread between two beads with a half-hitch knot. Pass through a few more beads, pull the thread taut, and snip close to beadwork (**figure 8**).

figure 8

9 Form the middle strand of this section by repeating steps 7 and 8 with two exceptions: Add one hex bead between the bicone and the 15° beads at each end; pass through the center hole of the three-strand connectors (**figure 9**).

figure 9

10 Form the outside strand of this section by repeating steps 7 and 8 with two exceptions: Add two hex beads between the bicone and the 15° beads at each end; pass through the outside hole of the three-strand connectors (**figure 10**). Set aside.

figure 10

11 Repeat steps 7 through 10 for the other side of necklace.

MAKING THE BACK SECTIONS

12 Thread a needle with approximately 18" (45.5 cm) of thread. Pick up one 3mm round, one hex bead, one bicone, and eight 15° beads. Leaving a 3" (7.5 cm) tail, pass through the inside hole of one of the three-strand connectors attached to the centerpiece, forming a loop of seed beads through this hole. Pass back through the bicone, hex bead, and 3mm round. Pull the threads taut and tie them together with an overhand knot (**figure 11**).

figure 11

13 *Pick up one hex bead, one bicone, one hex bead, and one 3mm round; repeat from * four more times. Pick up one hex bead, one bicone, and eight 15° beads. Pass through the inside hole of a three-strand reducer, forming a loop of seed beads through this hole. Pass back through all the beads between the connector and the reducer a couple of times. Tie the working thread around the thread between two beads with a half-hitch knot. Pass through a few more beads, pull the thread taut, and snip close to the beadwork **(figure 12)**.

figure 12

14 Form the middle strand of this section by repeating steps 12 and 13 with two exceptions: Add one hex bead between the bicone and 15° beads at each end; pass through the center hole of the three-strand connector and reducer.

15 Form the outside strand of this section by repeating steps 12 and 13 with two exceptions: Add two hex beads between the bicone and 15° beads at each end; pass through the center hole of the three-strand connector and reducer.

16 Use chain-nose pliers to open jump rings and attach the hook-and-eye clasp to the reducers **(figure 13)**.

figure 13

COORDINATING GEMSTONES

Gemstones come in many different colors, from the bright blue of sapphire to the deep red of garnet to the lustrous green of jade. The range of color and pattern within one type of stone is also quite varied.

Nouveau Tilework Necklace features amazonite beads of different sizes and shapes. The beads were purchased from two different shops, but, to ensure a perfect match, the first beads were on hand when the second purchase was made. The two amazonite beads pictured below show how varied same-named stones can be. When putting stones together for a piece of jewelry, it's best to select them up close and personal to get the perfect match.

Villa Igiea Palermo Necklace

Villa Igiea Mural

This mural, which graces the interior of Hotel Villa Igiea in Palermo, Sicily, was painted by architect Ernesto Basile, a master of the Italian Art Nouveau style. Born in Palermo in 1857, Basile created many public buildings and private villas in his hometown. Italy was the only nation to build its seat of government in the Art Nouveau style, and Prime Minister Giuseppe Zanardelli summoned Basile to Rome in 1899 to design the Palazzo del Parlamento.

(Stock Italia / Alamy)

ONE OF THE BEST THINGS ABOUT drawing beadwork inspiration from works of art is the surprise of discovering new color combinations. If not for the warm and rich use of mauve and topaz in this Italian mural, the two colors may not have found themselves together in a necklace. The flowers are typical of the Art Nouveau style and they're strung together on a latticework necklace that imitates the stripes in the maiden's dress.

FINISHED LENGTH:

20" (51 cm) long

TECHNIQUES:

peyote stitch, modified ladder stitch

MATERIALS AND TOOLS

· size 11° seed beads: 7 g lilac-lined amethyst, 1 g topaz matte

· size 11° cylinder beads: 1 g yellow-lined topaz AB

· 3–4mm drop beads (10), frosted topaz

· 4mm freshwater rice pearls, 6" (15 cm) strands (2)

· size 15° metallic gold seed beads (12) (optional)

· metallic gold lobster clasp (1)

· size D nylon beading thread

· wax or thread conditioner

· size 12 beading needle

· scissors

· clear nail polish

MAKING THE LARGE FLOWER

1 Thread a needle with approximately 3' (1 m) of thread and wax well. Pick up twenty-four cylinder beads and pass back through the second-to-last bead strung, forming a tip at the end **(figure 1)**.

figure 1

2 With amethyst seed beads, work one row of peyote stitch, ending by passing through the first bead strung. Turn and pass back through the last bead added **(figure 2)**.

figure 2

3 Continue making another row of peyote stitch, ending by passing back through the last bead added **(figure 3)**.

figure 3

4 Continue in this manner, adding one less bead to each subsequent row, until you have a row with five "up" beads **(figure 4)**.

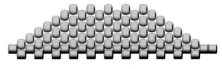

figure 4

5 Turn and pass through the first two up beads, do two regular peyote stitches, and pass through the first bead added in the previous row **(figure 5)**. Pull thread taut, causing the petal to curl.

figure 5

6 Weave the thread through to the other side of the center row, exiting the second bead opposite the tip end of the petal **(figure 6)**.

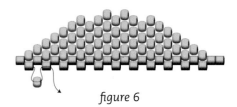

figure 6

7 Repeat steps 2 through 5 for the second side of the petal. Secure the thread but don't trim.

8 Repeat steps 1 through 7 until you have five petals.

9 Using the thread tails left from step 7, sew through the outer row of beads on two petals, joining the petals together from the center to about the mid point on each petal **(figure 7)**.

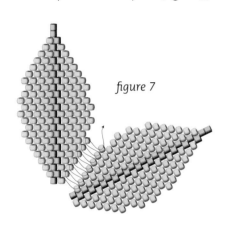

figure 7

10 Repeat step 9 until all five petals are joined.

11 Stitch a cluster of four drop beads to the center of the flower.

12 Secure the thread and trim. Dab the center back of the flower with clear nail polish.

MAKING THE SMALL FLOWERS

13 Repeat step 1 of the large flower, but pick up fourteen cylinder beads instead of twenty-four.

14 Repeat steps 2 and 3 of the large flower, ending with three up beads.

15 Turn and pass through the first two up beads, and then make one regular peyote stitch. Pull thread taut, causing the petal to curl.

16 Repeat steps 6 through 12 of the large flower, stitching three drop beads to the center of each flower instead of four, but do not dab the backs with nail polish.

MAKING THE DOUBLE-ROW NETTED CHAINS

17 Thread a needle with approximately 3' (1 m) of thread and wax well. With the thread exiting the fourth edge bead from the tip of a petal on the large flower and using 11° seed beads, pick up one amethyst, one topaz, one amethyst, one pearl, one amethyst, one topaz, and one amethyst.

18 Pass through the two beads to the left of the starting bead, through the starting bead, and through the first three seed beads and the pearl added in step 17 **(figure 8)**.

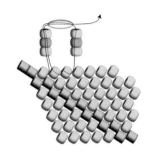

figure 8

19 Pick up one amethyst, one topaz, one amethyst, one pearl, one amethyst, one topaz, and one amethyst. Pass through the pearl added in the previous step and through the three seed beads added in this step **(figure 9)**.

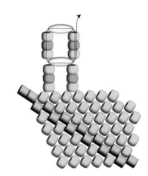

figure 9

20 Repeat step 19 until you have a chain with ten pearls.

21 To begin the next row, pick up one pearl, one amethyst, one topaz, one amethyst, and one pearl. Pass back through the second set of three seed beads along the edge of the first side of the chain **(figure 10)**.

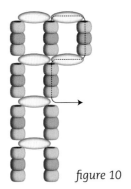

figure 10

22 Pick up one pearl, one amethyst, one topaz, and one amethyst. Pass through the second pearl and through the same set of three seed beads added in the previous step. Pass through the next set of three seed beads **(figure 11)**.

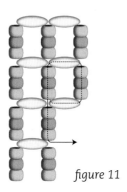

figure 11

23 Repeat step 22 along the length of the chain.

24 When you reach the flower, pass through the last set of three seed beads, and through three beads along the edge of the petal. Pick up one amethyst, one topaz, and one amethyst. Pass back through the last pearl added. Secure the thread and trim **(figure 12)**.

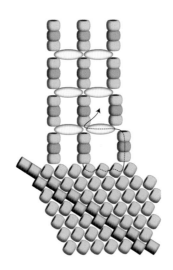

figure 12

25 Repeat steps 17 through 24 along the top edge of the opposite petal.

MAKING THE SINGLE-ROW CHAINS

26 With the thread exiting one of the top pearls of the double-row chain and the needle pointing toward the center of the chain, pick up one amethyst, one topaz, one amethyst, one pearl, one amethyst, one topaz, and one amethyst. Pass through the other top pearl of the double-row chain from the center toward the edge of the chain **(figure 13)**.

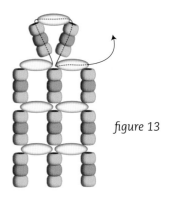

figure 13

27 Pass down through the next set of three seed beads, through the next pearl, and up through the center set of three seed beads. Pass through the first set of three seed beads added in step 26. Repeat step 19 of the double-row netted chain until you have a single-row netted chain with twenty-nine pearls **(figure 14)**.

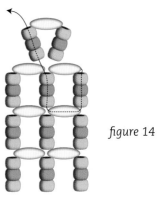

figure 14

28 Exiting the last pearl added, pick up one amethyst, one topaz, two amethyst, and three 15° beads. Pass through one end of the clasp. String three 15° beads and pass back through the last amethyst bead added. Pick up one amethyst, one topaz, and one amethyst bead and pass through the last pearl added. Pass through all these beads several more times to reinforce the connection **(figure 15)**.

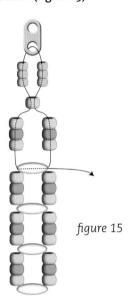

figure 15

Option: If you choose not to add the 15° seed beads, simply pass through the end of the clasp after stringing the four 11° seed beads, then pass back through the last seed bead added.

29 Repeat steps 26 through 28 for the other side of the necklace.

ATTACHING THE SMALL FLOWERS

30 Thread a needle with 18" (45.5 cm) of thread and wax well. Position a small flower over the juncture of double- to single-row chains. Sew the flower in place by passing through a bead in the flower, a bead in the chain, a bead in the flower, and so on until the flower is secure.

Note: If there is too much thread in the beads to pass through again, simply pass over the threads between the beads, moving to the next location with the thread between the flower and the chains.

COLOR SCHEMES

Villa Igiea Palermo Necklace plays off the most prominent color scheme in the mural—mauve and topaz accented with yellowish white and yellow—and the beads all end up having nearly equal prominence in the finished piece. The topaz beads that paint the flower spines are brighter than the rest, but they're used sparingly.

It can be difficult to see how the colors will work together while the beads are in their tubes. Try weaving a few beads together into little swatches to get a better idea of the overall effect. Here are some other possible color combinations that can be gleaned from Basile's mural.

stocking your stash

A beader's stash, or collection of beads and beading materials, often resembles a miniature bead shop, but you don't need a fully loaded beading arsenal to create the beaded projects in this book. You just need a few essentials, which you'll find listed in the Materials and Tools box at the beginning of each project. Rely on each list as your guide as you stock up for a specific project. Your beading stash will simply grow over time as you continue to make new projects.

The many bits and pieces available for creating beadwork are too numerous to mention, so we've provided brief descriptions of the specific items you'll need for the projects in this book. If you're an established beader, chances are you're quite familiar with and have many of these things on hand, but it never hurts to have a little review just to be sure you've covered all the bases. If you're new to beading, it's always good to know exactly what to ask for as you get busy stocking your stash.

BEADS

What we're here for! The love of beading starts with beads, from the sparkling crystal to the humble seed.

CRYSTAL BEADS are made of leaded glass—that is, glass that has been manufactured with lead oxide. The high lead content (up to 35 percent) causes the glass to refract light more than regular glass does. The most famous and sparkly crystals come from Austria, where top-secret machines cut the most precise, sharpest facets, adding to the dazzling light display. Beware of the holes in crystals because they are sharp and can easily cut thread. To prevent a potential beading disaster, add a seed bead to each side of the crystal to act as a buffer.

FIRE-POLISHED BEADS are made of leaded glass, too, but they don't have as high a lead content as the crystals described above. These beads are made in the Czech Republic, so they are sometimes called "Czech crystals." Although they aren't as sparkly as Austrian crystals, they are beautiful nonetheless—and a less expensive way to add shimmer to your beadwork.

PRESSED-GLASS BEADS are also produced in the Czech Republic. They are available in a staggering array of shapes, sizes, colors, and finishes. To make them, molten glass is poured into a mold. Typical pressed-glass beads include flowers and leaves, but also available are rounds, ovals, squares, pyramids, barrels, and other novelty shapes (such as cat faces and skulls).

LAMPWORKED BEADS are one of the oldest types of glass beads. They're made by heating a cane of glass over a torch and then winding the hot glass onto a metal wire. This is a relatively crude process for making beads, as the results aren't uniform, but this technique has had a huge renaissance in the last decade, and skilled artisans have brought the craft to a new artistic level. Also called "art beads," because they're individually made, lampworked beads are available in a variety of glass types and finishing techniques, which makes each bead unique.

METAL BEADS are made with all kinds of metals. The most common are sterling and fine silver, brass, gold filled, and vermeil (which is made by adding a 24-karat gold coating over a sterling silver base bead). Metal beads come in a wide array of shapes, so they make great accents when combined with more colorful beads. They also make a strong statement on their own.

PEARL BEADS are natural mollusk-produced beads. The most common types found in bead shops are the freshwater variety, most likely from China, although Japan and India produce them in large quantities, too. Pearl farmers insert either a shell or plastic base into a mollusk. The mollusk makes itself more comfortable by secreting a smooth coating, or nacre, over this base. Different mollusks produce different-colored pearls, but some pearls are dyed. If you buy dyed pearls, ask the salesperson if the color will rub off. If so, leave them at the store—or, when you get home, give them a light coat of clear acrylic spray paint. Pearls usually have small holes, so you'll need to use thin wire or stitch with a thin beading needle when working with them.

RESIN BEADS are made with high-quality translucent plastic that looks much like etched glass. They are very durable and come in a variety of shapes.

SEED BEADS are so named because of their diminutive size. They are made by first heating glass and pulling it into a long cane, then blowing a hole down the center of the cane. The cane is chopped into little pieces and heated or tumbled to soften the edges.

Seed beads come in all different sizes, from the size of a pomegranate seed to a celery seed. The size is indicated by an "aught," or °. The larger the bead, the smaller the aught number. The most common sizes are between 15° and 6°.

Seed beads come primarily from the Czech Republic and Japan. *Czech seed beads* have slightly smaller holes than the Japanese kind and are somewhat irregular in shape.

Japanese seed beads are very uniform and have a bit wider hole.

Cylinder beads are another type of Japanese seed bead. They are extremely uniform, have thin walls, and also have a very wide hole.

All seed beads come in a wide range of colors, finishes, and cuts. For example, a size 13° or 14° Czech seed bead with facets is called a *charlotte*. A size 12° Czech seed bead with one facet is called a *true cut*. A Japanese seed bead with six sides is called a *hex*, and Japanese seed beads with three sides are called *triangles*.

There are other glass, seedlike beads out there, too, including drops and bugles. Although they aren't officially labeled as seed beads, they're made in much the same way. You'll find them in the seed-bead section of the bead store. *Drops*, sometimes called fringe beads or magatamas, look like size 6° seed beads with an off-center hole. These work well for embellishing fringe.

Bugles are about the same width as a size 10° seed bead, but are much longer and are often faceted. Beware—they have sharp edges. (As when working with crystals, a good habit to prevent a beading catastrophe is to use a seed bead at each end to act as a buffer.)

Shell beads are made out of the shiny coating found inside a shell, which is called nacre or mother of pearl. Each mollusk species creates its own color and pattern of nacre, and, as a result, shell beads come in a wide variety of types.

Stone beads are made out of just about any type of stone you can think of, including rubies and diamonds. They come from all over the world, and vary in price depending on the value of the stone. Many stone beads are round, but you will also find rondelles, ovals, and other shapes including donuts. Tumbled-stone nugget and chip beads are also very popular. When you buy stone beads, inquire about whether they've been dyed or not. A surface dye will eventually fade, so even though they might look pretty at the store, you might want to leave dyed beads out of your shopping tray.

Sequins, although frequently found in fabric shops, are beads, too! (Technically, anything with a hole through it qualifies as a bead.) Sequins are made of plastic and are available in every color imaginable. Beaders find endless ways to embellish their work with sequins, and the vintage varieties are especially sought after.

Wood beads are among the first types of beads humans ever made! Found in every type of wood, they are often dyed, carved, or even laminated to create layered effects. Many of the wood beads that are available in the United States come from Asia and South America.

FINDINGS

Like a wooden truss, door handle, or the stained-glass windowpanes of a grand hotel or cathedral, findings are what support, open and close, and sometimes embellish your beaded jewelry.

Buttons are great for decorating pieces, but they can also function as closures for a loop/button clasp.

Chain serves as necklace straps, holds bead dangles together, or simply embellishes your jewelry. You'll be surprised by the wide variety of link shapes and sizes. You might want to consider using individual chain links as decorative jump rings—just use two pairs of chain-nose pliers to open each link (page 83).

Clasps are the closures you'll need to finish off a necklace, bracelet, or anklet. There are dozens of different types. In this book we've primarily used three types of clasps: box clasps, hook-and-eye clasps, and toggle clasps.

Box clasps have a springy metal tab on one side. The other side has a metal box into which you place the tab.

Hook-and-eye clasps are shaped as their name describes and are closed by hooking into a jump ring or chain.

Toggle clasps consist of a ring and a bar—just slip the bar through the ring, turn the bar 90 degrees, and the bar lies across the ring, securing the piece.

Connector bars come in a variety of shapes and sizes. They are handy for keeping multiple strands in a piece of jewelry neat.

CRIMP BEADS AND CRIMP TUBES are tiny metal beads that secure flexible beading wire to findings. Sterling silver or gold-filled crimp beads or tubes work the best. See page 84 for instructions on how to crimp. Be sure to use crimping pliers (page 83) to achieve the most professional-looking results.

EAR WIRES are used to attach earring dangles to pierced ears. The most common, French ear wires, are shaped like a **J,** but there are several other types to choose from, too.

EYE PINS are thin pieces of wire that have a loop at one end. They are often used to make bead links.

HEAD PINS consist of a thin wire with a flat, perpendicular disk at one end. In jewelry making, they're most often used to create dangles.

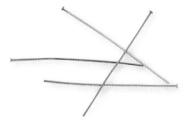

JUMP RINGS are so named because of their function— they act as a link, or "jump," from one section of a piece of jewelry to another. They are made up of circles or ovals of wire, often with a slit on one side that can be opened and closed with chain-nose pliers. See page 91 for the proper technique for opening and closing jump rings.

PIN BACKS are great when you want to turn a piece of beadwork into a brooch or pin. They usually have a flat metal portion onto which you sew the work and a levered pin on the back that's secured by a spring-loaded closure.

STRINGING MATERIALS

Just as a painter needs a canvas, you need a good strong base onto which to work your beaded art. Stringing materials are the backbone of a beaded piece, so don't skimp when it comes to quality. Although threads and wires might not be the most exciting part of the piece, they're holding it all together, so take care to get the best type.

NYLON BEADING THREAD is made up of dozens of thin strands of nylon twisted together. It comes in a wide array of colors, so it's easy to match this type of thread to a project—the thread disappears into the work. It's best to prepare nylon thread with wax or thread conditioner (page 82) to prevent it from tangling or fraying.

BRAIDED BEADING THREAD is a material borrowed from the fishing industry. It's made with miniscule synthetic fibers, braided together to make an extremely strong thread. It comes in several "tests," a classification that refers to how many pounds it can handle without breaking. The 6-lb. test variety works great for most beadwork projects.

Braided beading thread only comes in white, moss green, and clear, but the limited choice in colors is a small trade-off for such a hearty, nonabrading stringing material. (If you feel you really need to have it all, buy white braided thread and color it with a permanent marker in the color of your choice.) Braided beading thread cuts best with inexpensive craft scissors, not the sharp embroidery kind.

FLEXIBLE BEADING WIRE is made up of twisted strands of stainless steel wire that are coated with nylon. It generally comes in three widths—fine, medium, and heavy—and a wide range of colors, including sterling silver coated and 24-karat gold coated. This wire is not the once-popular "tiger tail" beading wire—it drapes like silk and is resistant to kinks.

METAL WIRE is used in this book for creating decorative wrapping (*Métro Station Earrings*, page 22), creating bead links (*Scheherazade Necklace*, page 56), and dangles (*Nouveau Tilework Necklace*, page 62). Metal wire is measured in "gauges" or widths. The smaller the gauge number, the thicker the wire. It comes in every sort of metal imaginable, but solid sterling silver and gold filled are the two most practical types for jewelry.

These precious metals don't stain the skin (like brass does), are very strong (unlike copper), and are forgiving (unlike plated wires, which snap easily). If you are just learning wirework, practice on some inexpensive copper wire instead.

OTHER HANDY MATERIALS

When stocking your stash, you'll focus most of your attention on beads, string, and findings. To complete your toolbox, however, you'll still need a few other items.

BEADING MATS are indispensable to have when you're working with seed beads. They keep the beads stable on the work surface so they don't roll around or bounce to the floor. The best type of mat is made with Vellux fabric, but a piece of terry cloth, chamois, or felt works well, too.

GLUES secure beadwork to findings and seal knots. *Industrial-strength clear adhesive* is the strongest glue, but very smelly. Be sure to use it in a well-ventilated area.

Jeweler's or *watchmaker's cement* is used for lighter-weight projects and dries clear.

If you only need to seal a knot, you can travel no further than your nail care drawer. *Clear nail polish* works wonders.

FELT is used as a base for bead embroidery. The stiff type works the best, as it has a limited amount of "fuzz" and will help keep the beadwork firm.

LEATHER OR ULTRASUEDE makes a good base for bead embroidery. For the projects in this book, we use it as a backing to hide stitches.

WAXES AND THREAD CONDITIONERS are used to pre-coat beading thread. *Beeswax* keeps the thread from fraying and tangling. Some beaders also like the fact that the sticky wax fills up seed beads, stiffening their beadwork. *Microcrystalline wax*, a synthetic form of beeswax, works much the same way.

Thread conditioner keeps thread from fraying and tangling, too, but isn't used for stiffening beadwork. Actually, thread conditioner is much like hair conditioner—it makes the thread soft and silky.

TOOLS

Finally, you'll need to have a good set of tools to get the job done. Buying tools is another time to avoid frugality. A good set of tools will yield years of service and few headaches, making them worth the investment.

BEADING NEEDLES generally come in two varieties: English beading needles and sharp needles. *English beading needles* are very thin and come in variable lengths—up to 3" (7.5 cm).

Sharp needles are shorter and thicker than English beading needles. They work great for stitched beadwork because their length makes them easy to maneuver.

Most beadwork projects call for a size 10 to size 13 needle, but needles come in an assortment of sizes. The smaller the number, the thicker the needle.

SCISSORS are a necessity when creating beadwork with thread. Sharp, pointed *embroidery scissors* work best with projects made with nylon thread.

Children's craft scissors are best for cutting braided beading thread.

PLIERS come in a variety of styles, but there are only three that are must-haves for the projects in this book. *Chain-nose pliers* have jaws that are flat on the inside, rounded on the outside, and taper to a point. They're used for making sharp wire bends and grasping and wrapping wire, but also come in handy for pulling beading needles out of a too-full bead.

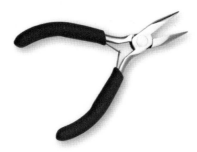

Crimping pliers have notched jaws used to secure crimp beads and crimp tubes to flexible beading wire (page 84).

Round-nose pliers have tubular jaws that come to a point and are used for bending wire into curves and loops.

WIRE CUTTERS are used to cut metal wire. One side of the cutters makes a flat, or flush, cut. The other side will make a V-shaped cut. Buy cutters that are meant for jewelry making only. Those with a pointed tip are usually your best bet. And never use your "good" cutters to cut flexible beading wire—the stainless steel is tough on the blades.

beading know-how

Beadworkers have a wide array of techniques to work with—from simple to complex, functional to experimental. This chapter doesn't include all your choices, of course, but here's a brief guide to the techniques you'll need to know in order to complete the projects in this book.

BEGINNING AND ENDING THREADS

When you have only about 4" (10 cm) of thread left on your needle, tie it off by making a half-hitch or overhand knot between the beads, then pass through a few beads, and pull the thread taut to hide the knot inside a bead. Trim the thread close to the beadwork.

To begin a new thread, pass through a few beads, tie a half-hitch knot between the beads, then pass through a few more beads, and pull the thread taut to hide the knot inside a bead. Trim the tail close to the beadwork.

When you have two thread tails to tie together, use a square knot.

CRIMPING

Working with pliers made especially for this purpose, you'll fold crimp beads or tubes around beading wire to secure the wire to a clasp or connector.

1. String beads to the point where you want to add a clasp. Pass the wire through a crimp bead or tube, through the ring of the clasp, back through the crimp tube, and (if possible) back through a few of the last beads strung.

2. Pull the wire to snug the beads up against the clasp. Making sure the wires are lined up side by side in the tube, use the first (inner) notch of the pliers to squeeze the tube around the wires.

3. Turn the tube on its side and place it into the second (outer) notch of the pliers. Squeeze the tube to form it into a rounded cylinder.

FRINGE

Fringe adds dimension and decorative edge-finishing to your beadwork. You can work with one strand or hundreds, depending on the final look you want.

1. Exiting your beadwork base, string the number of beads you want in your fringe. Skipping the last bead, pass back through the remaining beads just added and back into the beadwork base.

2. Repeat as desired.

HERRINGBONE STITCH

Herringbone stitch produces a fabric of beads that looks like multiple two-row columns of beads positioned in V formations.

1. Make a foundation row with ladder stitch (page 86), using an even number of beads.

2. With the thread exiting up through the last bead of the foundation row, string two beads and pass down through the next bead in the foundation (the second-to-last bead of the row) and up through the bead after that (the third-to-last bead of the row).

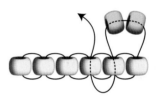

3. *String two beads and pass down through the next bead of the foundation row and up through the follow-ing bead. Repeat from * to the end of the row and pass back through the last bead of this row.

4. Continue adding rows by repeating step 3, stringing two beads and passing down and then up through two beads of the previous row.

TUBULAR HERRINGBONE STITCH

This stitch produces a tube that can stand alone, be strung with other elements, or be embellished with fringe.

1. Make a foundation row with ladder stitch (at right) that is a multiple of two beads long and either one or two beads high. Join the ends of this foundation row together to form a circle.

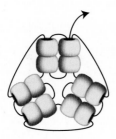

2. *String two beads and pass down through the next bead and up through the following bead. Repeat from * to the end of the round.

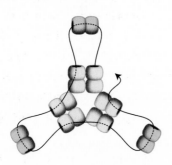

3. At the end of the round, pass through the first bead of the previous and the current round to step up into position to begin the next round.

4. When you have finished the tube, tighten and secure the last round by passing through the beads in ladder-stitch fashion.

LADDER STITCH

Ladder stitch makes a straight strip of beadwork and is often used to create a foundation row from which to work other stitches. It can be one bead wide or can be made with stacked bead columns.

1. String two beads and pass through both beads again. Adjust the beads so their sides touch.

2. *String one bead and pass through the last bead stitched and this new bead again. Repeat from *, adding one bead at a time, until the strip is your desired length.

LOOMWORK

Loomwork is great for quickly making long strips or large pieces of beaded fabric. The downside is that once you've finished the weaving, you'll have many thread ends to secure and weave back into the work. The threads that are attached to the loom are called warp threads. The threads holding the beads are weft threads.

1. Warp the loom with one more warp thread than the number of beads in the width of your project. Thread a needle with a comfortable length of thread. Leaving a 6" (15 cm) tail to be woven in later, tie the thread to the first warp thread about 6" (15 cm) from the end of the loom.

2. String the beads for the first row of your pattern. Holding the threaded needle, bring these beads under and across the warp threads. Use the index finger of your free hand to push the beads up so there is one bead between each pair of warp threads.

3. Bring the threaded needle over the warp threads and pass back through each bead back to the beginning of the row. Be careful not to pierce any threads as you pass back through the beads.

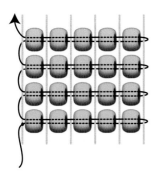

4. Continue adding rows in this manner until you have completed your pattern.

LOOMWORK INCREASES

You can increase only to the number of warp threads available on either side of your main piece, so plan your shaping in advance. You could add warp threads as necessary, but increasing is easier if they are already in place.

To increase at the end of a row, simply add the number of beads desired and finish the row as usual.

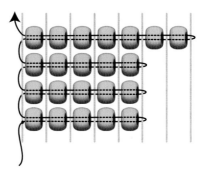

To increase at the beginning of a row, bring the weft thread under, over, then under the warp thread next to the last bead. String the number of beads desired for the increase, push them up between the warp threads, and then bring the weft over the warp thread next to the last bead and through the top of all the increased beads. Pass the thread back under the warp and finish the row as usual, passing through the increased beads again.

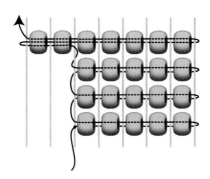

LOOMWORK DECREASES

To decrease at the end of a row, simply string the desired number of beads and bring the weft thread to the top after the warp thread next to the last bead.

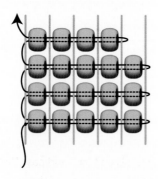

To decrease at the beginning of the row, bring the weft thread under the outer warp thread and pass through the number of beads to be decreased. Bring the weft thread under, over, and under the next warp thread and proceed as usual.

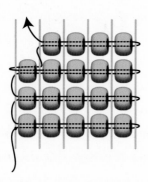

PEYOTE STITCH

Peyote stitch produces a beaded fabric in staggered rows that are stacked in bricklike fashion.

EVEN-COUNT FLAT PEYOTE STITCH

1. String an even number of beads to the width that you want your piece to be. These beads will form the first two rows.

2. String one bead, skip one bead, and pass through the second-to-last bead of the original beads strung.

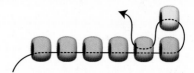

3. *String a bead, skip a bead, and pass through the next bead. Repeat from * to the end of the row.

4. Once you have finished this row, every other bead will be sticking up slightly—the "up" beads. On subsequent rows, pick up a bead and pass through the next up bead.

PEYOTE STITCH DECREASES

For a decrease at the beginning of a row, weave through the beads to exit from the spot you want to start the new row and continue stitching. For an end-of-row decrease, simply stop adding beads and begin the new row.

To make a mid-row decrease, stitch to the place where you want to make the decrease, pass the thread through two beads without adding a bead. In the next row, add one bead above the decrease.

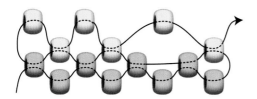

PEYOTE STITCH INCREASES

When you get to the place where you want to increase, string two beads and pass through the next up bead. In the next row, add one bead between the two beads added. You can do this at the end of a row or mid-row.

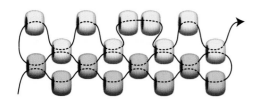

EVEN-COUNT TUBULAR PEYOTE STITCH

1. String an even number of beads for the desired circumference. Pass through all of the beads twice more, pulling the thread tight to form a ring.

2. *String a bead, skip a bead, and pass through the next bead. Repeat from * to the end of the round.

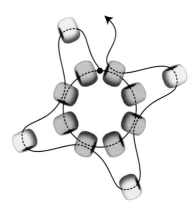

3. At the end of the round, pass through the first bead added in this round to "step up" into position to begin the next round.

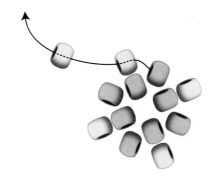

SPIRAL STITCH

This stitch produces a rope of beads, wherein the outer beads spiral around an inner core. You can work with any size beads—just be sure that the outer set is never shorter then the core. This example uses 8° beads for the core and size 11° beads for the outer spiral.

1. String four 8° beads and five 11° beads. Pass through the four core beads again.

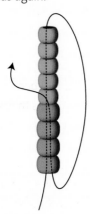

2. String one core bead and five outer beads. Pass through the last three core beads and the core bead just strung.

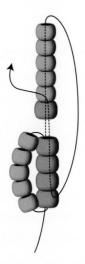

3. Repeat step 2 to desired length.

SQUARE STITCH

This stitch is unique among the off-loom techniques in that the beads are aligned in a perfectly even manner from side to side and top to bottom. The resulting fabric of beads looks the same as loom-woven beads.

1. String a row of beads the desired width of the piece. String one bead, pass through the last bead of those initially strung, and pass through the new bead again.

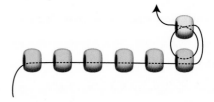

2. *String a bead, pass through the next bead in the row below and again through the bead just strung. Repeat from * to the end of the row. Add more rows in this looping manner until your piece is the desired size.

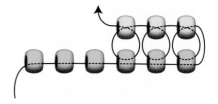

SQUARE STITCH DECREASE

Weave through the last row and exit from the bead where you want the next row to begin.

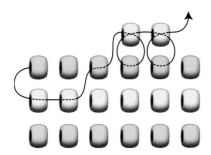

SQUARE STITCH INCREASE

At the end of the row, string the number of beads you want to increase and work them as for a first row, then continue across the row in the usual manner.

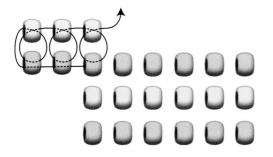

STRINGING

The most important thing to consider when stringing is pairing your beads with an appropriate stringing material. We recommend specific materials for each project, but in general you should select the strongest material that will fit through the holes in your beads.

Do not try to pick up a bead and put it onto your needle or stringing material. Rather, use your needle or the end of your wire to scoop a bead up from your work surface.

WIREWORK

The topic of wirework could be a book in itself! Here are a few simple wirework techniques that we've used in these projects.

OPENING AND CLOSING LOOPS AND JUMP RINGS

Use two pairs of chain-nose pliers to grasp the ring on either side of the place where the wires meet and gently twist one side up and one side down. Slip your connecting piece onto the loop and close with the reverse motion.

SIMPLE LOOP

1. Using chain-nose pliers, make a 90-degree bend in the wire ⅜" to ½" (1 to 1.5 cm) from the end.

2. With round-nose pliers, grasp the end of the wire. Holding firmly onto the body wire, slowly turn the pliers to form a loop in the end of the wire. Continue turning until the end of the wire meets the body wire.

SPIRALS

Use round-nose pliers to make a small loop at one end of a wire. Grasp the loop with chain-nose pliers so it sits flat within the jaws. Use your thumb to push the wire along the side of the loop. Adjust the loop within the pliers so you can continue pushing the wire, creating a larger spiral.

WRAPPED LOOP

1. Using chain-nose pliers, make a 90-degree bend in the wire 2" (5 cm) from the end.

2. With round-nose pliers, grasp the wire at the bend. Use your fingers to wrap the short end of the wire up and over the top of the pliers. Change the pliers' jaw position so the bottom jaw is inside the loop. Swing the short wire end under the bottom jaw.

3. Use your fingers or chain-nose pliers to grasp the short wire end. Wrap the end tightly down the neck of the wire to form several coils.

4. Trim the excess close to the coils.

WRAPPING

You can tightly wrap or coil wire to attach one wire to another or to create decorative coils. Start by grasping the base wire tightly in one hand. Hold the wrapping wire with your other hand and make one wrap. Reposition your hands so you can continue to wrap the wire around the base wire, making tight revolutions.

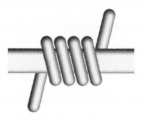

online bead sources

We like to shop at our local bead shops as much as possible—to help ensure that they'll be there when we need them! Here are a few online sources that we also sometimes use.

Artbeads.com > www.artbeads.com

The Bead Goes On > www.beadgoeson.com

The Bead Monkey > www.thebeadmonkey.com

The Beadin' Path > www.beadinpath.com

Beyond Beadery > www.beyondbeadery.com

Bobby Bead > www.bobbybead.com

Caravan Beads, Inc. > www.caravanbeads.com

Cartwright's Sequins > www.ccartwright.com

Dakota Stones > www.dakotastones.com

Fire Mountain Gems and Beads > www.firemountaingems.com

Natural Touch Beads > www.naturaltouchbeads.com

Ornamental Resources, Inc. > www.ornabead.com

Queen Beads > www.queenbeads.com

Rio Grande > www.riogrande.com

Shipwreck Beads > www.shipwreckbeads.com

Soft Flex Company > www.softflexcompany.com

Star's Clasps > www.starsclasps.com

Whole Bead Shop > www.wholebeadshop.com

further reading

Ayers, Andres. *The Architecture of Paris*. Fellbach, Germany: Edition Axel Menges, 2004.

Battersby, Martin. *The World of Art Nouveau*. New York: Funk & Wagnalls, 1968.

Derville, Frank. "Art Nouveau World Wide." http://perso.orange.fr/artnouveau/en/index.htm

Gustav Klimt: A Poster Book. New York: Harmony Books, 1976.

Kirk, Terry. *The Architecture of Modern Italy: Visions of Utopia, 1900–Present*.
New York: Princeton Architectural Press, 2005.

MyStudios.com. "Artist Snapshots." Barewalls Interactive Art.
www.mystudios.com/bios

Revi, Albert Christian. *American Art Nouveau Glass*. Camden, New Jersey:
Thomas Nelson & Sons, 1968.

Schmutzler, Robert. *Art Nouveau*. New York: Harry N. Abrams, 1962.

Spinzia, Judith A. "Artistry in Glass: The Undisputed Master, Our Oyster Bay Neighbor,"
The Freeholder: Magazine Online, Oyster Bay Historical Society, 1997.

Thorne, J. O., and T. C. Collocott, eds. *Chambers Biographical Dictionary*, rev. ed.
Edinburgh: W & R Chambers, 1984.

The Columbia Electronic Encyclopedia, 6th ed. New York: Columbia University Press, 2007.

3d-dali.com. "Biographies of Painting Masters."
www.3d-dali.com/Artist-Biographies/Biographies.html

acknowledgments

Huge thanks go out to all the beaders, designers, authors, and teachers we've encountered over the years—you provide inspiration to keep us going. Thanks to Linda Ligon of Interweave Press for having given us really cool jobs that allowed us to meet each other and advance our beading know-how.

Very special thanks go to Julia S. Pretl, Beading Goddess, whom we were blessed with having as our illustrator and technical editor. Her pictures speak a thousand words. Thanks to the staff at Creative Publishing international, including creative director Rosalind Wanke for providing the guiding light, art director Sylvia McArdle for putting all the pieces together, project manager Ellen Goldstein for directing traffic, and, most especially, editor Deborah Cannarella for encouraging us to get together and write some books.

about the authors

JUDITH DURANT is author of *Ready, Set, Bead* (Creative Publishing international, 2007) and *Never Knit Your Man a Sweater (unless you've got the ring)* (Storey, 2006); editor of *One-Skein Wonders: 101 Yarn Shop Favorites* (Storey, 2006) and *101 Designer One-Skein Wonders* (Storey, 2007); and coauthor, with Jean Campbell, of *The New Beader's Companion* (Interweave, 2005) and *Beadwork Inspired by Art: Impressionist Jewelry and Accessories* (Creative Publishing international, 2008). She is a former craft book editor for Interweave Press and has edited dozens of books on beadwork and knitting. She has contributed designs and articles to *Interweave Knits, Beadwork,* and *PieceWork* magazines and had a regular column in *Beadwork* for five years. She lives with her husband in Lowell, Massachusetts.

JEAN CAMPBELL is an editor and author with a hankering for beads. She is the founding editor of *Beadwork* magazine and has written and edited more than forty books, most recently including *The New Beader's Companion* (Interweave, 2005) and *Beadwork Inspired by Art: Impressionist Jewelry and Accessories* (Creative Publishing international, 2008), both with Judith Durant. She is also the author of *Beaded Weddings* (Interweave, 2006), *The Art of Beaded Beads* (Lark, 2006), *Beadwork Creates Jewelry* (Interweave, 2007), and *Beading with Crystals* (Lark, 2007). Jean has appeared on the DIY channel's *Jewelry Making* show, *The Shay Pendray Show,* and PBS's *Beads, Baubles, and Jewels,* where she gives how-to instructions, provides inspiration, and lends crafting advice. She is a certified Precious Metal Clay instructor and teaches off-loom beading and metal clay workshops throughout the United States. She lives with her husband and two children in Minneapolis, Minnesota.